Connect with English

CONVERSATION BOOK 4

Pam Tiberia
Janet Battiste
Michael Berman
Linda Butler

McGraw Hill

Boston, Massachusetts   Burr Ridge, Illinois   Dubuque, Iowa   Madison, Wisconsin
New York, New York   San Francisco, California   St. Louis, Missouri
Bangkok   Bogotá   Caracas   Lisbon   London   Madrid   Mexico City
Milan   New Delhi   Seoul   Singapore   Sydney   Taipei   Toronto

McGraw-Hill

A Division of The **McGraw·Hill** *Companies*

CONNECT WITH ENGLISH: CONVERSATION BOOK 4

This book is printed on acid-free paper.

domestic 1 2 3 4 5 6 7 8 9 0 QPD QPD 3 2 1 0 9 8
international 1 2 3 4 5 6 7 8 9 QPD QPD 3 2 1 0 9 8

ISBN 0-07-292767-4

Editorial director: Thalia Dorwick
Publisher: Tim Stookesberry
Development editor: Pam Tiberia
Marketing manager: Tracy Landrum
Production supervisor: Richard DeVitto
Print materials consultant: Marilyn Rosenthal
Project manager: Gayle Jaeger, Function Thru Form, Inc.
Design and Electronic Production: Function Thru Form, Inc.
Typeface: Frutiger
Printer and Binder: Quebecor Press Dubuque

Grateful acknowledgment is made for use of the following:

Still Photography: Jeffrey Dunn, Ron Gordon, Judy Mason, Margaret Strom

Additional Photographs: Episode 37 – page 4: © UPI/Corbis-Bettmann; *Episode 45 – page 5:* © Superstock; *page 6:* © Siegried Layda/Tony Stone Images; *Appendix 3 –* © Superstock ; *Appendix 11 – left to right:* © UPI/Corbis-Bettmann; © UPI/Corbis-Bettmann

Illustrations: Episode 37 – page 2: Steve Stankiewicz; *Episode 38 – page 3:* Amy Wummer, *page 5 and page 6:* Steve Stankiewicz; *Episode 39 – page 4:* George Reimann; *Episode 40 – page 2:* Amy Wummer, *page 3:* Steve Stankiewicz, *page 5 and page 6:* Amy Wummer; *Episode 41 – page 5:* Steve Stankiewicz; *page 6:* Andrew Shiff; *Episode 42 – page 1:* George Reimann; *Episode 43 – page 3:* Andrew Shiff; *Episode 44 – page 2 and page 6:* Steve Stankiewicz; *Episode 45 – page 1:* Steve Stankiewicz, *page 2:* George Reimann; *Episode 47 – page 2 and page 3:* Steve Stankiewicz; *Episode 48 – page 1:* Steve Stankiewicz; *Appendix 13:* Steve Stankiewicz

Special thanks to Deborah Gordon, Robin Longshaw, Cheryl Pavlik, and Bill Preston for their contributions to *Conversation Books 1–4*.

Library of Congress Catalog Card No.: 97-75580

International Edition

When ordering this title, use ISBN 0-07-115910-X.

http://www.mhhe.com

Table of Contents

To the Teacher

The primary goal of each *Conversation Book* is to help students develop oral communication skills using the themes found in **Connect with English** as a springboard for classroom discussion. This introduction and the following Visual Tour provide important information on how each *Conversation Book* and the corresponding video episodes can be successfully combined to teach English as a second or foreign language.

LANGUAGE SKILLS:

Each *Conversation Book* has 12 chapters which contain a variety of pair, group, team, and whole-class activities that are based on important issues and ideas from the corresponding video episodes.

The activity types vary with each chapter but generally include an assortment of role-plays, discussions, opinion surveys, games, interviews, and question-naires. In each chapter, a special two-page section is devoted to longer games, information gaps, and songs from the **Connect with English** sound-track. Students also have the opportunity to work on special project pages found in appendices in the back of the book. These projects provide students with the opportunity to explore key themes outside of the classroom.

THEMATIC ORGANIZATION:

Events and issues that are familiar and important to all ESL/EFL learners have been purposely included in the **Connect with English** story. These topics were carefully chosen for their relevant cultural content, and they provide a rich context for the communicative activities found in the *Conversation Books*. As students watch the video story and become familiar with the events and characters, the *Conversation Books* provide a framework within which students can freely discuss the ideas presented in each episode. Throughout *Conversation Books 1-4,* students are given the opportunity to explore such varied themes as the following:

- Pursuing Your Dream
- Making Future Plans
- Looking for a Job
- Making New Friends
- Money vs. Love
- Having Fun
- Apologizing
- Making a Difficult Decision
- Gossip
- Divorce and Remarriage
- Regrets
- Anger

- Making Compromises
- Spending Money
- Adulthood
- Best Friends
- Managing Priorities
- Parenting
- Helping Others
- The Death of a Loved One
- Dedication
- Moving
- Holidays
- Life Lessons

PROFICIENCY LEVEL:

The activities found in each *Conversation Book* are designed for use with high-beginning to intermediate students. Special icons are used to identify the difficulty level of each activity in the book. These icons help teachers tailor the activities for the needs of students at different levels of language proficiency.

 Arrows pointing up indicate that the difficulty of an activity can be increased.

 Arrows pointing down indicate that an activity can be simplified.

 Arrows pointing in both directions indicate that the difficulty level of the activity can be either increased or simplified.

Detailed teaching suggestions on modifying each activity are found in the accompanying Instructor's Manual.

OPTIONS FOR USE:

The *Conversation Books* are specifically designed for classroom use. While it is assumed that students have watched the corresponding video episode at least once before attempting the activities in the book, it is not necessary to have classroom access to a TV or VCR. Teachers may choose to show the video during class time, or they can assign students to watch the video episodes prior to class, either in a library, language lab, or at home. Class time can then be used for completion of the activities found in the *Conversation Book*.

Each *Conversation Book* can be used as the sole text in any course that emphasizes oral communication skills. Teachers also have the option of combining the *Conversation Books* with other corresponding texts in the **Connect with English** print package:

■ *Video Comprehension Books 1-4* contain a variety of comprehension activities that enhance and solidify students' understanding of main events in the video story.

■ *Grammar Guides 1-4* provide multilevel practice in grammar structures and vocabulary items derived from the **Connect with English** video episodes.

■ *Connections Readers* (16 titles) offer students graded reading practice based on the **Connect with English** story.

■ *Video Scripts 1-4* include the exact dialogue from each of the video episodes and can be used in a variety of ways in conjunction with any of the other texts in the **Connect with English** program.

For additional information on these and other materials in the **Connect with English** program, please refer to the inside back cover of this book.

A VISUAL TOUR OF THIS TEXT

This visual tour is designed to introduce the key features of *Conversation Book 4*. The primary focus of each *Conversation Book* is to help students develop oral communication skills within the context of the *Connect with English* story. *Conversation Book 4* corresponds to episodes 37-48 of *Connect with English*, and it presents an assortment of activities dealing with various aspects of communication, including explaining, questioning, interviewing, reporting, paraphrasing, describing, stating feelings/opinions, and more.

Themes drawn directly from the video episodes are listed at the start of each chapter. In Episode 42, activities are based on the themes of Waiting, The Importance of Education, and An Audition. A two-page activity is devoted to the song "Dream Catcher," and an optional project focuses on the theme of Dedication.

Variety of Activity Types
Each chapter contains a variety of activity types that feature different student combinations and communicative objectives. For example, Activity 1 features a brainstorming activity to be done as a class, while Activity 2 contains a group survey in which students collect and synthesize information.

Conversation Book 4 often features a logical progression of activities. For example, a partner interview about waiting in Activity 3 is followed by an analysis of interview responses in Activity 4. This organization reinforces important concepts and vocabulary and provides an additional opportunity to discuss various issues evolving from each theme.

Activities such as discussions and opinion surveys invite students to share personal experiences and opinions as they relate to the themes from the video story. In Activity 5, students discuss their ideas about the importance of education.

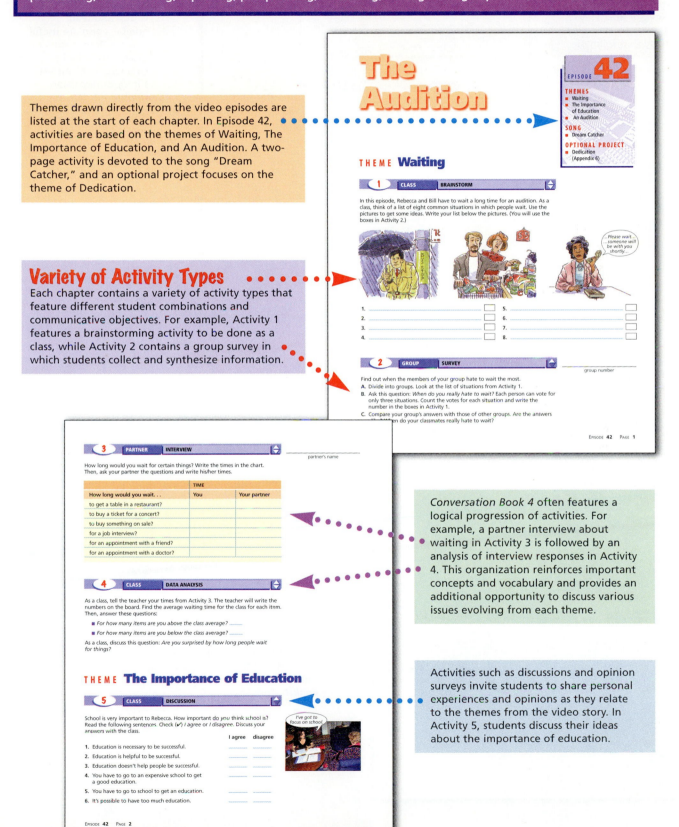

Activity bars identify the start of each numbered activity and indicate whether the activity is designed for pairs, groups, teams, or whole-class participation. Descriptors such as **Discussion, Interview,** or **Role-Play** alert teachers to the type of activity that follows.

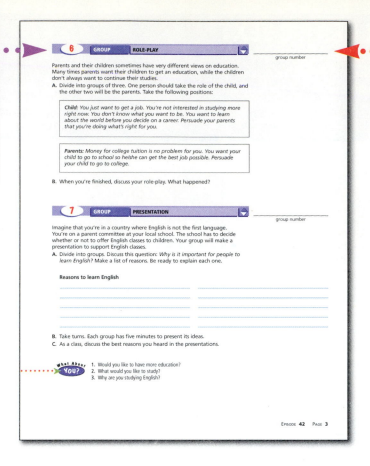

Spaces that allow students to indicate partner name, group number, and team number make it easier for students and teachers to keep track of student collaborations. Group and team numbers also are useful when different student groups are asked to compare and contrast survey or discussion results with one another.

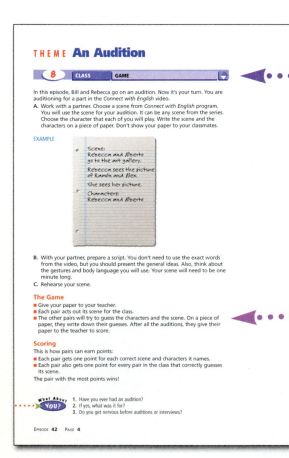

Multilevel Activities

Special icons are used to show the difficulty level of each activity in the book. These icons are designed to help teachers tailor the activities to the needs of a multilevel group of students. An arrow pointing up ◆ indicates that the difficulty of an activity can be increased, while an arrow pointing down ◆ indicates that an activity can be simplified for lower-level students. Arrows pointing in both directions ◆ indicate that the activity can be adjusted in either direction. Detailed teaching suggestions for how to change the level of each activity in *Conversation Book 4* are included in the accompanying Instructor's Manual.

This interactive game based on the concept of auditions simultaneously encourages communication among pairs of students and the larger class, and also serves to be a timely review of previous events from the ***Connect with English*** story.

Two-Page Activity

Each episode contains an extended theme which is covered in a longer, two-page activity. These themes are developed into games, information gaps, or activities based on songs from the *Connect with English* soundtrack.

Rebecca's song "Dream Catcher" provides the basis for this two-page activity. In all activities involving songs from the *Connect with English* soundtrack, the lyrics are presented to the students for purposes of review and discussion.

Comprehension and interpretation questions bring students close to the content of the song lyrics, and prepare them for subsequent activities.

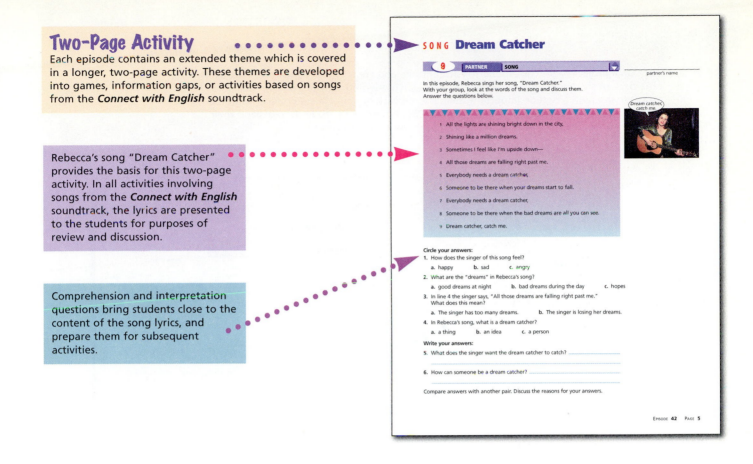

SONG **Dream Catcher**

9 | PARTNER | SONG

partner's name

In this episode, Rebecca sings her song, "Dream Catcher." With your group, look at the words of the song and discuss them. Answer the questions below.

Dream catcher, catch me.

1 All the lights are shining bright down in the city,
2 Shining like a million dreams.
3 Sometimes I feel like I'm upside down—
4 All those dreams are falling right past me.
5 Everybody needs a dream catcher,
6 Someone to be there when your dreams start to fall.
7 Everybody needs a dream catcher,
8 Someone to be there when the bad dreams are all you can see.
9 Dream catcher, catch me.

Circle your answers:
1. How does the singer of this song feel?
   a. happy   b. sad   c. angry
2. What are the "dreams" in Rebecca's song?
   a. good dreams at night   b. bad dreams during the day   c. hopes
3. In line 4 the singer says, "All those dreams are falling right past me." What does this mean?
   a. The singer has too many dreams.   b. The singer is losing her dreams.
4. In Rebecca's song, what is a dream catcher?
   a. a thing   b. an idea   c. a person

Write your answers:
5. What does the singer want the dream catcher to catch? _____

6. How can someone be a dream catcher? _____

Compare answers with another pair. Discuss the reasons for your answers.

EPISODE **42**   PAGE **5**

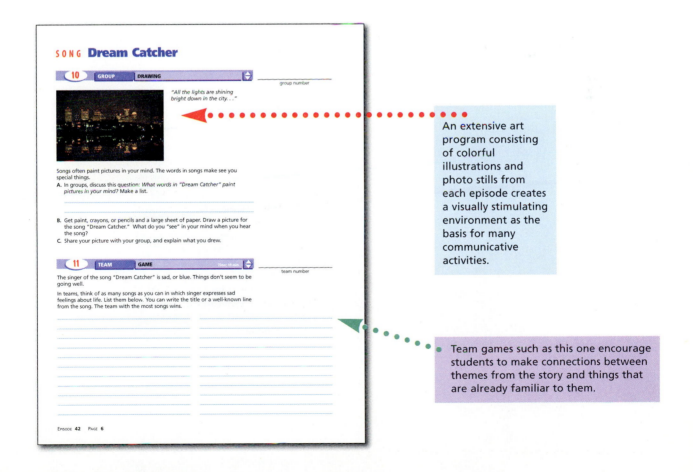

SONG **Dream Catcher**

10 | GROUP | DRAWING

group number

"All the lights are shining bright down in the city. . ."

Songs often paint pictures in your mind. The words in songs make see you special things.
A. In groups, discuss this question: *What words in "Dream Catcher" paint pictures in your mind?* Make a list.

B. Get paint, crayons, or pencils and a large sheet of paper. Draw a picture for the song "Dream Catcher." What do you "see" in your mind when you hear the song?
C. Share your picture with your group, and explain what you drew.

11 | TEAM | GAME

team number

The singer of the song "Dream Catcher" is sad, or blue. Things don't seem to be going well.

In teams, think of as many songs as you can in which singer expresses sad feelings about life. List them below. You can write the title or a well-known line from the song. The team with the most songs wins.

EPISODE **42**   PAGE **6**

An extensive art program consisting of colorful illustrations and photo stills from each episode creates a visually stimulating environment as the basis for many communicative activities.

Team games such as this one encourage students to make connections between themes from the story and things that are already familiar to them.

Project Page

Optional project pages correspond to each episode and are found in appendices located at the back of the book. Project pages contain research-oriented activities or community surveys and polls based on important themes from each episode. These projects reinforce the communicative nature of the *Conversation Books* and invite students to expand their learning and conversation to areas beyond the classroom environment.

Project pages throughout the *Conversation Books* encourage students to use a variety of research tools, including books, encyclopedias, newspapers, magazines, almanacs, and the Internet.

On this project page, students are invited to research the lives of well-known people who were dedicated to a certain cause or field of study. Many times, students will be asked to make a class presentation, which serves the dual purpose of solidifying their own knowledge of the material and successfully communicating it to their classmates.

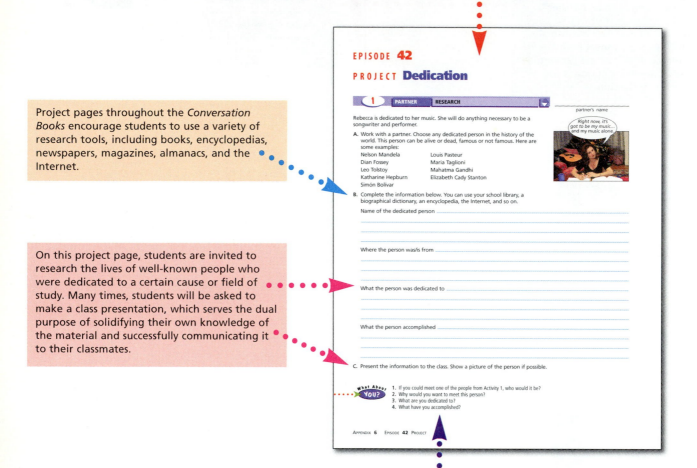

What About You? activities provide open-ended questions that encourage students to express their personal feelings and opinions as they relate to the themes from the story. These activities create a springboard for more sophisticated discussions among students who are at higher levels of oral proficiency. **What About You?** activities can also be used as optional writing assignments.

Thanksgiving

EPISODE 37

THEMES
- Family Holidays
- Family Secrets
- Thanksgiving Day

GAME
- Thanksgiving Football

OPTIONAL PROJECT
- Computer Classes (Appendix 1)

THEME Family Holidays

1 CLASS BRAINSTORM

cook

play games

sing

Look at the photos above. They show things the Casey family did on Thanksgiving. As a class, make a list of things families do on holidays. Think about the Casey family. Think about your family. For example, do you tell family stories? Do you talk about the past? Your teacher will write your list on the board.

2 PARTNER INTERVIEW

_____
partner's name

A. Write five things your family does on holidays. Use the list from Activity 1 for ideas.

B. Interview your partner. Ask your partner this question: *What does your family do for family holidays?*

C. Write your partner's answers. How many of your answers are the same?

Your answers

1. _____
2. _____
3. _____
4. _____
5. _____

Your partner's answers

1. _____
2. _____
3. _____
4. _____
5. _____

Uncle Tim

The family members below are coming to your house for a holiday dinner.

A. Read the descriptions of each person.

B. With your group, discuss where each person should sit at the table above. Write each person's name next to a chair at the table. One name is done for you. *Note: There is more than one way to seat people around the table.*

Dad: He smokes.

Uncle Tim: He wants to sit at one end of the table.

Aunt Betty: She wants to sit across from Jane.

Grandpa Joe: He doesn't like little children.

Cousin Jane: She doesn't like smoke.

Cousin Peter: He is seven years old.

Mom: She doesn't like Aunt Betty.

You: You want to sit next to Peter.

C. When you've finished, compare your answers with those of other groups. Do your tables look the same? Talk about which table is the best.

 **What About YOU?**

1. What holidays do you and your family celebrate together?
2. Do you usually cook something for family holidays?
3. How are family holidays like other parties? How are they different?
4. Do you ever travel far for family holidays?

THEME Family Secrets

4 | **PARTNER** | **ROLE-PLAY**

_____
partner's name

In this episode, Rebecca learns a family secret.

With a partner, write a dialogue for one of the following situations. Practice the dialogue. Then, present it to the class.

Why didn't you and my father talk for so many years? What happened?

Situations

- At your family house, you find an old picture of your mother. In the picture, your mother is kissing a man. The man is not your father. You ask about it.
- Your father has lived in the same house for 20 years. You have never seen him go down to the basement. You think this is very strange. One day, you ask him about it.
- Your sister buys an expensive new car. The next week, she rents a nice apartment. You don't understand where the money is coming from. You ask her about it.
- Your mother never talks about her parents. One day, you ask her about them.

THEME Thanksgiving Day

5 | **PARTNER** | **MAKING GUESSES**

_____
partner's name

Thanksgiving Day celebrates an important event in the history of the United States. Make guesses about the dates and times of the historical events below. Use the clues in the box. You will read a story in Activity 6 and see how close your guesses are.

	Your guess	Actual date	Difference
1. When was the first Thanksgiving?	_____	_____	_____
2. When was the first national day of thanksgiving in the United States?	_____	_____	_____
3. When did Thanksgiving become an official holiday?	_____	_____	_____
4. When did the day of Thanksgiving become the fourth Thursday in November?	_____	_____	_____

Total difference: _____

CLUES

► George Washington, the first president of the United States, called for the first national day of prayer and thanksgiving.

► Because of Franklin Roosevelt, Thanksgiving is always on a Thursday. He was president during the bad economic times of the 1930s.

► The Pilgrims celebrated the first Thanksgiving. They came to the new land in 1620.

► President Abraham Lincoln made Thanksgiving an official holiday. He lived during the 1800s.

A. Read the following story.

The Story of Thanksgiving

In 1620, a group of people from Europe arrived in what is now Massachusetts. They wanted to make a home in this new land. These people were called Pilgrims. They were the first people who spoke English to come and stay in what is now the United States.

The Pilgrims had a long, hard journey across the Atlantic Ocean. There were 102 people on a small ship. It took 65 days for the ship to cross the sea.

When they arrived, they had an even worse time. It was winter. Many of the Pilgrims died before the spring.

The Pilgrims had to learn how to live in the new land. They got help from a group of Native Americans called the Wampanoags. These Native Americans taught the Pilgrims how to hunt, fish, and grow food. A Native American named Squanto was very helpful to the Pilgrims. He spoke some English!

That first year, the Pilgrims grew a lot of food, and they were thankful. So, in 1621, the Pilgrims celebrated the first Thanksgiving with the Wampanoags. It was a celebration of the food and of their success. They had a feast with turkey, corn, beans, and other foods.

Over 150 years later, George Washington, the first president of the United States, decided to made November 26, 1789, a day of thanksgiving and prayer. It was first national day of thanksgiving. In 1863, President Abraham Lincoln made Thanksgiving an official national holiday. It was to be celebrated every year in November. Finally, in 1939, President Franklin Roosevelt changed Thanksgiving Day to the fourth Thursday of November.

B. Retell the story to your partner from Activity 5. Do not look back at the story. Try to tell the important events. Also tell the most interesting fact you learned.

C. Your partner will retell the story to you. Check (✔) the information that he/she says.
❏ who the Pilgrims were
❏ what the Pilgrims learned from the Native Americans
❏ why the Pilgrims wanted to celebrate
❏ what they did to celebrate
❏ when Thanksgiving became an official holiday

D. Go back to Activity 5. Fill in the correct dates. Find the difference between your guesses and the real dates. Then, find the total difference. Finally, compare your answers with those of other pairs. Which pair has the smallest total difference?

1. Is there a holiday of thanksgiving in your country?
2. If there is, what do people do on the thanksgiving day?
3. What is an important event in the history of your country? Tell the story.
4. What are you most thankful for?

G A M E **Thanksgiving Football**

The American version of football is one of the most popular sports in the United States. On Thanksgiving Day, there are many football games on television. In football, two teams move up and down a field. One team moves toward one side of the field, the other team moves to the other side. When a team comes to the end of the field (crosses the goal), it scores (makes a touchdown). The field is divided into yards. (A yard is about 1 meter.)

In this game, your team moves up and down the field when it answers questions correctly.

Get Ready to Play

Step One

Divide into two teams. One is team A and the other is team B. Each team will write 20 questions about the *Connect with English* story. Write each question on a separate piece of paper. After each question, write 10, 20, or 30 in parentheses ( ). These are the number of yards a team will move when it answers the question.

About this episode:

What is one food the Casey family eats on Thanksgiving? (20)

What is the game Kevin and the girls play outside on Thanksgiving? (10)

About the story:

What is the name of Rebecca's school? (20)

What is Alberto's job? (30)

Step Two

Give your questions to your teacher. He/she will read the questions and check them over. Your teacher will also write some questions about the story.

Play the Game

- Each team uses a different coin as a marker. Place them at the 50-yard line. Flip a coin to see which team starts.
- The teacher picks a question at random and reads it to the team. If a team answers correctly, it moves its coin toward its goal line. The coin should be moved forward the number of yards written on the card.
- If a team answers incorrectly, it moves its coin *away* from its goal line. The coin should be moved backward the number of yards written on the card. *Note: Team A moves toward Team A's goal line. Team B moves toward Team B's goal line.*

EXAMPLE

What is the name of Rebecca's school? (20)

If a team answers this question correctly, it moves its coin 20 yards toward its goal line. If a team doesn't answer this question correctly, it moves its coin 20 yards away from its goal line.

- Each team has a chance to answer three questions on every turn.
- Every time a team gets to the goal line, it scores a touchdown. Then the team starts over again at the 50-yard line. If a team doesn't score a touchdown on its turn, it starts over again at the 50-yard line on its next turn.
- The first team to score three touchdowns wins!

TEAM **A** GOAL LINE

10 · 20 · 30 · 40 · 50 YARD LINE · 40 · 30 · 20 · 10

TEAM **B** GOAL LINE

Starting Over

EPISODE **38**

THEMES
- Christmas Bonuses
- Giving Advice
- Losing a Job

INFORMATION GAP
- Decorating a Christmas Tree

OPTIONAL PROJECT
- Sports for Children (Appendix 2)

THEME Christmas Bonuses

 1 | **GROUP** | **SURVEY**

In this episode, Alberto receives a Christmas bonus. His boss gives him two opera tickets.

A. Write your name in the first line of the chart. Next to your name, write the Christmas bonus that you would like to get. You can use the ideas below, or some of your own.

Kinds of Christmas Bonuses
- tickets to a sports game or a concert
- a basket of food
- a gift certificate for a store or a restaurant
- a day off
- money

B. Divide into groups. Ask your group members this question: *What Christmas bonus would you like to get?* Write their answers in the chart.

group number

Name	What Christmas bonus would you like to get?
You:	
1.	
2.	
3.	
4.	
5.	
6.	

Join another group. Compare your answers from Activity 1.

A. Count the total number of people who chose each of these Christmas bonuses. Write the number in the spaces below.

_____ tickets to a sports game or a concert

_____ a basket of food

_____ a gift certificate for a store or a restaurant

_____ a day off

_____ money

Which is the most popular answer? _____

B. List three other ideas for Christmas bonuses.

1. _____

2. _____

3. _____

C. How many people in your group have ever gotten a Christmas bonus? _____

3   GROUP   **DISCUSSION**

_____
group number

Divide into groups. Your group is the board of directors for a company.
Your company has had a good year. You are having a meeting about Christmas bonuses for the employees of your company. Discuss and answer the questions below. When your group finishes, present your answers to the class.
Explain your decisions.

1. Which employees will get Christmas bonuses? Check (✔) your answer.

_____ only full-time employees who did great work this year

_____ all full-time employees

_____ all full-time and part-time employees

_____ only full-time and part-time employees who did great work this year

_____ Nobody will get bonuses.

2. What kind of bonus will you give your employees? Check (✔) your answer.

_____ money

_____ a gift (tickets to the opera, for example)

_____ money and a gift

3. If you give money, how much will you give to each person? _____

4. If you give a gift, what will it be? _____

THEME Giving Advice

 4 | **PARTNER** | **WAYS TO SAY IT**

In this episode, Rebecca needs to start over in San Francisco. She needs to go back to school and work. Nancy gives Rebecca advice.

Here are some ways that people give advice:

You should get more rest.	**You ought to** get a job.
If I were you, I'd go to bed.	**Why don't you** apply for a scholarship?

Work with a partner. Look at the situations below. Take turns. One person chooses a situation. The other person gives some advice. Then, make up your own situation.

EXAMPLE Student A: I have a headache.   Student B: You should take some aspirin.

Situations   **Expressions**

1. I need money for a college course.   _____

2. I have a bad cold.   _____

3. My wallet was stolen.   _____

4. I feel very stressed and anxious.   _____

5. Your situation: _____

 5 | **GROUP** | **DISCUSSION**

A. Divide into groups. Read the following information about Harry. Talk about his problems. Decide what advice to give him. Write your ideas on a separate piece of paper.

This is Harry. He's a very nice guy, but his life is a mess. Here are some of Harry's problems:

- He hates his job, but he needs money.
- His roommate got married and moved out. Now Harry is paying all the rent for a two-bedroom apartment.
- He thinks his girlfriend is in love with another man.
- His brother borrowed his car last week. He hasn't brought it back.

B. Join another group. Compare your advice for Harry. Discuss what is best for Harry to do.

 What About YOU?

1. When was the last time you asked someone for advice? What was it about?
2. Who do you usually ask for advice? Why do you ask that person?
3. Do you like to give advice?

THEME Losing a Job

group number

In this episode, Rebecca learns she has lost her job. Rebecca was away from work because of her father's death, so her boss hired a new person. Did Rebecca's boss do the right thing?

A. Your teacher will divide the class into three groups. Groups 1 and 2 will debate. Group 3 decides the winner of the debate.

B. Read the directions for each group.

Group 1

Your position: *People can't expect their employers to give them time off for family problems.* Talk about the reasons for this position. Write them down. Prepare to present your reasons.

Group 2

Your position: *Employees shouldn't lose their jobs because they need time off for family problems. Laws should protect them.* Talk about the reasons for your position. Write them down. Prepare to present your reasons.

Group 3

During the debate, take notes on good ideas. After the debate, choose the winner. Decide: *Which team presented the best ideas?*

C. Groups 1 and 2 take turns presenting their positions. Then Group 3 meets to decide which group gave the best presentation. Group 3 announces its decision.

D. The whole class votes on this question: *Do you agree with Position 1 or Position 2?*

---

7 | PARTNER | DISCUSSION

partner's name

Rebecca has lost her job. She needs to find a new one. Which of the jobs above do you think would be best for her?

A. Work with a partner. Discuss the three jobs. Look at all of the information in each advertisement. Decide which job would be best for Rebecca. Be ready give your reasons to the class.

B. Write the number of the best job. _____

C. As a class, discuss the good and bad points of each job. Take a class vote: *Which job would be best for Rebecca: 1, 2, or 3?*

PARTNER | **INFORMATION GAP**

STUDENT A | Work with a partner. One of you works on this page. The other works on page 6. Don't look at your partner's page.

Nancy Shaw decorates her Christmas tree in the same way every year. First, she puts on lights. Then, she hangs ornaments. These ornaments have been in her family for a long time.

You can see some of the ornaments on the tree in the picture below. Your partner has more ornaments in his/her picture of the tree. Make your trees match. *Note: You can see all the kinds of ornaments in the small pictures below. Some ornaments are on the tree in two places.*

A. Tell your partner what you can see hanging on the tree. For example, say: *In the first row of ornaments, there is a candy cane on the right.*

B. Find out what's missing. For example, ask, *What's next to the candy cane?* Write the names of the missing ornaments in the right places.

C. When you're finished, compare trees with your partner. Are they the same?

an angel   a present   a cookie

a bell   a reindeer   a star

a candle   a snowflake   a glass ball

a candy cane   a snowman   a stocking

STUDENT B | Work with a partner. One of you works on this page. The other works on page 5. Don't look at your partner's page.

Nancy Shaw decorates her Christmas tree in the same way every year. First, she puts on lights. Then, she hangs ornaments. These ornaments have been in her family for a long time.

You can see some of the ornaments on the tree in the picture below. Your partner has more ornaments in his/her picture of the tree. Make your trees match. *Note: You can see all the kinds of ornaments in the small pictures below. Some ornaments are on the tree in two places.*

A. Tell your partner what you can see hanging on the tree. For example, say: *On the bottom row of ornaments, there is a reindeer on the right.*

B. Find out what's missing. For example, ask, *What's next to the reindeer?* Write the names of the missing ornaments in the right places.

C. When you're finished, compare trees with your partner. Are they the same?

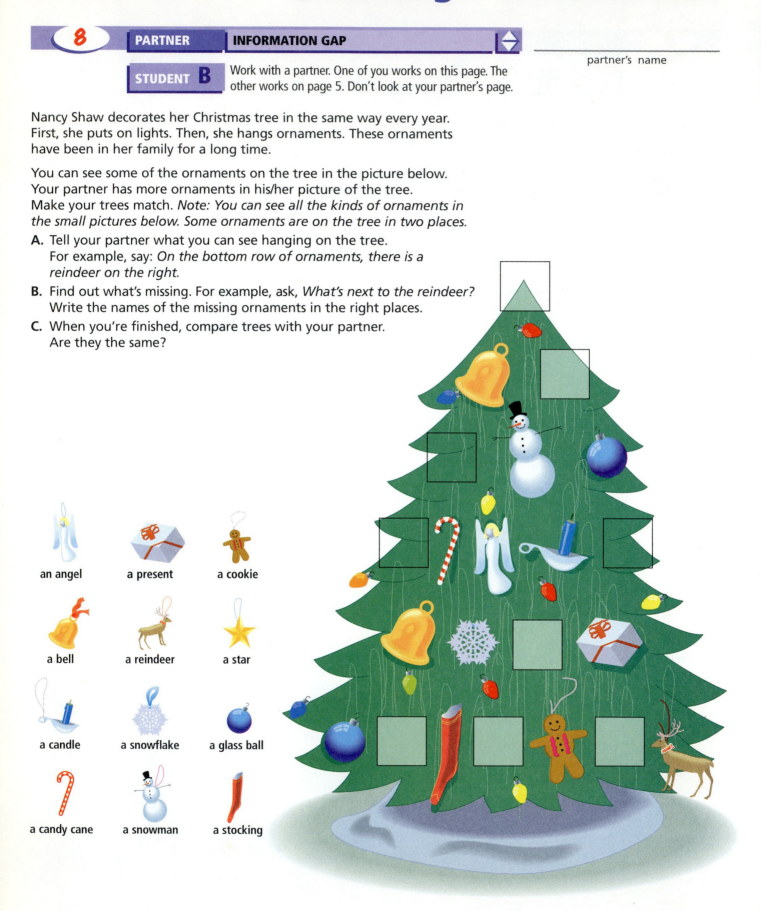

an angel   a present   a cookie

a bell   a reindeer   a star

a candle   a snowflake   a glass ball

a candy cane   a snowman   a stocking

The Pressure's On

EPISODE **39**

THEMES
- Managing Priorities
- Stress
- Being Direct

GAME
- Studying for Exams

OPTIONAL PROJECT
- Opera (Appendix 3)

T H E M E Managing Priorities

 1   **GROUP**   **DISCUSSION**

group number

In this episode, Rebecca has too much to do. She must *manage her priorities*, and decide what things she must do first. Help Rebecca manage her priorities for one evening.

A. Divide into groups. Read the situation.

Situation

It's Tuesday night. Rebecca has a big final exam tomorrow. She knows that she needs to study three hours for it. She has to look over her notes from class. Also, she wants to get to bed by 11 o'clock. She doesn't want to feel tired during the exam tomorrow morning.
Things Rebecca has to do on Tuesday nights: ■ do the laundry   ■ write her brother a letter   ■ help Nancy clean the kitchen ■ practice the guitar   ■ pay bills
When Rebecca arrives home from school at 4 o'clock, she finds these things: ■ a note from Nancy: It says that the rent is due today.   ■ a message from an old friend: She's visiting San Francisco for only one night. She's at a hotel waiting for Rebecca's call. ■ a message from Alberto: He wants Rebecca to go to a party tonight.

B. Discuss the situation. What things should Rebecca do on Tuesday night? Decide on her *priorities*. Make a list, with number 1 as the most important thing.

1. _____   4. _____

2. _____   5. _____

3. _____   6. _____

C. What should Rebecca do about the things that aren't on the list in Part B? For example, if she isn't able to go to the party, should she call Alberto and tell him? Discuss your ideas with the group.

1. Are you good at managing priorities? Why or why not?
2. What are your three most important priorities in life?
3. What were your three most important priorities five years ago?

THEME Stress

_____
partner's name

school	politics	work	your health	your family
your car	money	your apartment/house	your social life	your future

In this episode, Rebecca has a lot of stress. She has to pass her exams! Look at the list above. Circle the three things that give you the most stress and write them below. Ask your partner the question: *What three things give you the most stress?* Write your partner's answers. Are your answers alike?

Your answers

1. _____
2. _____
3. _____

Your partner's answers

1. _____
2. _____
3. _____

3 PARTNER STRESS TEST

_____
partner's name

Take the "Stress Test" below. Check (✔) *Often*, *Sometimes*, or *Never*. Then ask your partner the questions below, and check (✔) your partner's answers. Discuss the results.

	YOU			YOUR PARTNER		
	Often	Sometimes	Never	Often	Sometimes	Never
1. Do you feel you have too much to do?						
2. Do you worry about school or work?						
3. Do you get angry with people easily?						
4. Do you feel tired and nervous?						
5. Do you think that people expect too much of you?						

Scoring: ***Often*** answers are worth 2 points.
   Sometimes answers are worth 1 point.
   Never answers are worth 0 points.

If your score is between 0–4 points: Don't worry. You're calm.

If your score is between 5–7 points: You're in the middle. But try to take more time to relax!

If your score is 8 points or more: You're stressed. Look at Activity 4 for ways to relieve stress!

4 GROUP SURVEY

A. Ask the members of your group this question: *What do you do to relieve stress?* Write their answers. Here are some ideas for ways to relieve stress: exercise, talk with friends/relatives, listen to music, watch TV, meditate, and take breaks from work.

Name	What do you do to relieve stress?

B. Share results as a class. Then, in your group, discuss these questions:
- *What is the most popular way to relieve stress?*
- *What is the most unusual way?*
- *Which new way would you try?*

THEME Being Direct

5 PARTNER WAYS TO SAY IT

In this episode, Professor Thomas is *direct* with Rebecca. He tells her clearly that her exams will be difficult. Here are some ways that people are direct in English. These are ways to begin a sentence:

To be frank, your exams are going to be tough. Real tough.

To be frank,...	To be perfectly honest,...	I don't want to lie to you, but...
To tell you the truth,...	Truthfully,...	If you want the truth,...

Work with a partner. Look at the situations below. One person chooses a situation. The other person chooses an expression from the box above. Take turns. Then, make up your own situation.

EXAMPLE   Student A: Do you like my new jacket?   Student B: To be honest, I don't like it.

Situations

Expressions

1. Does my music bother you?

2. I'm sorry I didn't meet you yesterday. Are you angry?

3. I was wondering. How much money do you make?

4. Do you like my new outfit?

5. Your situation:

In some situations, people prefer to be direct. For example, you would be direct if you want to be very clear about how you feel. In other situations, people prefer to be indirect. You might be indirect if you want to be more careful about what you're saying. Discuss the following situations with your partner. For each case, decide if it's best to be *direct* or *indirect*. Check (✔) your answers.

DIRECT		INDIRECT

1. Two friends who share an apartment

2. A husband and a wife

3. Hosts and their guests at a party

4. A proud mother and her friend

What About YOU?

1. Are you usually direct or indirect with people?
2. Is it better to be direct or indirect with people?
3. In what situations is it better to be direct?

GAME **Studying for Exams**

You're studying for an exam. If you study the right way, you'll pass the exam!

Get Ready to Play

Step One
Divide into groups of two to four players. Each group needs a coin.

Step Two
Each player will make at least six game cards. Game cards look like these:

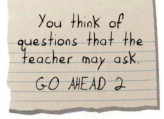
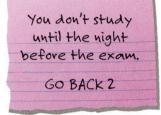
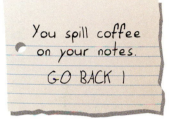

Each game card should have either a good or a bad way to study. Good ways to study should say GO AHEAD. Bad ways to study should say GO BACK. Make each card for one or two spaces. You can work alone or with others to make the game cards. Here are some ideas:

Good Ways to Study	Bad Ways to Study
■ You study a few hours every day before the test. ■ You work with a classmate, and ask each other questions. ■ You make a list of important words and their meanings.	■ You stay up all night before the test. ■ You lose your notes. ■ You drink four cups of coffee the night before the exam and can't sleep.

Step Three
Make sure no two game cards are exactly the same. Shuffle the game cards and put them in a pile face down on the table. Turn to the game board on page 6. Cut out the markers on Appendix 13. Put your marker on START.

Play the Game
■ Decide who will go first. That player tosses the coin. If it lands heads up, the player moves ahead one space. If it lands tails up, the player moves ahead two spaces.
■ If there's something written on the space where you land, read the words aloud. Follow the directions. You may have to move ahead, move back, or draw a card.
■ If you draw a card, read it aloud. Follow the directions on the card. You can draw only one card on each turn.
■ If the card tells you to move AHEAD or BACK to a space, move your marker and stay there. Don't follow the directions on that space. Wait for your next turn.
■ If you land on a FREE space, stay there, and wait for your next turn.
■ The next player tosses the coin, and play continues. The first person to reach YOU PASSED! passes the exam and wins the game.

GAME Studying for Exams

START	

RETURN TO START

You forget your textbook.

TAKE A CARD

FREE

GO AHEAD 1
You read over your textbook.

TAKE A CARD

You study with a friend. You can answer all his/her questions.
GO AHEAD 1

TAKE A CARD

GO AHEAD 1
You write down important ideas in your own words.

TAKE A CARD

FREE

TAKE A CARD

GO BACK 1
You lose your notebook.

TAKE A CARD

FREE

GO BACK 1
You fall asleep studying.

TAKE A CARD

TAKE A CARD

You look up words you don't know in the dictionary.
GO AHEAD 1

YOU PASSED!

TAKE A CARD

TAKE A CARD

FREE

GO AHEAD 1
You read an extra book on the topic.

TAKE A CARD

Sharing Feelings

EPISODE **40**

THEMES
- Things That Are Important to You
- Being Patient or Impatient
- Making Money

INFORMATION GAP
- Rock and Roll Music

OPTIONAL PROJECT
- Using the Library (Appendix 4)

THEME Things That Are Important to You

 GROUP | **RANKING**

_____
group number

People have different ideas about what's important in life.

A. First, work on your own. What's important to you? Rank the items on the list below. Write 1 for most important and 10 for least important.

_____ having a nice house

_____ getting a college education or a graduate school education

_____ having a family

_____ being rich

_____ having lots of friends

_____ traveling to many different countries

_____ having an important job

_____ doing good things for the community

_____ being famous

_____ doing lots of interesting things (crafts, music, sports, and so on) in your free time

① *Rock is where the money is these days.*

② *Money isn't all that important to me.*

B. Share your lists in groups. Answer these questions:
- *Are there any items in the top three on everyone's list?* List them.

_____

_____

_____

- *Are there any items in the bottom three on everyone's list?* List them.

_____

_____

_____

A. Are there any items you'd like to add to the list in Activity 1? Write three ideas on the lines below.

B. Interview your partner. Ask this question: _What other things are important to you in life?_

C. Write your partner's ideas. Did any of your partner's answers surprise you?

Your ideas	Your partner's ideas
1. _____	**1.** _____
2. _____	**2.** _____
3. _____	**3.** _____

THEME   Being Patient or Impatient

3   **CLASS**   **BRAINSTORM** ⬎

In what situations are you impatient? Are you impatient when you wait in line? Are you impatient in traffic? Are you impatient when you try to learn new things?

As a class, make a list of some situations when people are impatient. Write your answers on a separate piece of paper. Your teacher will write a "master list" on the board.

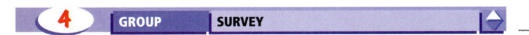

4   **GROUP**   **SURVEY** ⬍

_____
group number

A. Divide into groups.

B. Ask the people in your group this question: _In what situation are you the most impatient?_ Write their answers. Use the list from Activity 3 or your own ideas.

Name	In what situation are you the most impatient?
1.	
2.	
3.	
4.	

5 GROUP DISCUSSION

In many cultures, it's a good thing to be patient. Do you think it's ever good to be impatient? For example, is it good to be impatient in a store? Is it good to be impatient with family or friends? Is it good to be impatient in an emergency?

A. Divide into groups. Make a list of three times when it's good to be patient, and three times when it's good to be impatient.

B. Share your lists with another group.

Times to be patient	Times to be impatient
1. _____	1. _____
2. _____	2. _____
3. _____	3. _____

What About YOU?

1. Are you a patient or impatient person?
2. What's better in your country, being patient or impatient?
3. Can you learn to be more patient? If so, how?

THEME Making Money

6 PARTNER BRAINSTORM

Most people would like to make money, but they don't always know how to do it. Work with your partner to think of at least three ways for people to make money. Write your ideas below. Give details! Don't just say, "Open a business." Tell the kind of business. Don't just say, "Invent something." Tell the kind of invention.

_____

_____

_____

_____

_____

_____

_____

_____

_____

_____

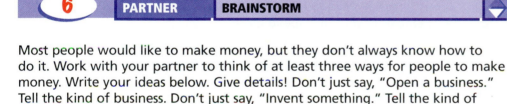

A Business

An Investment

An Invention

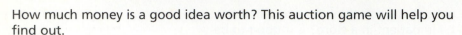

7   **TEAM**   **GAME**   Time: 15 min.

How much money is a good idea worth? This auction game will help you find out.

A. Work with your partner from Activity 6. Form teams with one or two other pairs. Decide on the five best ideas that your team had in Activity 6.

B. Write your team number and your ideas on a large piece of paper. Post your paper on a wall in your classroom.

C. In this game, your team and other teams will offer money for the ideas on the walls. These offers of money are called "bids."

The Game

Your team will win if it is the team with the most money at the end of the game. This is how your team will earn money:

> ■ Your team gets all the money that the other teams bid on your ideas.
>
> ■ Your team gets all the money it offers for an idea, but only if your team's bid was the *highest*.

Your team has $600 to spend on three good ideas from other teams. You can't bid on any ideas from your own team's paper. Remember: Your team needs to spend more than other teams in order to get the best ideas.

■ Read each paper on the wall. With your team, decide which three ideas to bid on. Do *not* let other teams know your choices.

■ Write down the three ideas your team wants to bid on. Also write the amount of money you want to spend on each idea. Remember you can't spend more than $600 in total.

Ideas to bid on	How much money you'll spend
1. _____	_____
2. _____	_____
3. _____	_____

■ Copy your bids onto a separate piece of paper. Your teacher will collect them when the time is up. Your teacher will also figure out your team's score. Remember—your score is a combination of the following:
  ▶ the amount of money other teams paid for your ideas
  ▶ the amount of money your team spent if it was the highest bidder on an idea

The team with the most amount of money wins!

1. What's the quickest way to make money?
2. Do you need to go to college to make a lot of money?
3. Do you want to make a lot of money? Why or why not?

INFORMATION GAP **Rock and Roll Music**

 8 | **PARTNER** | **INFORMATION GAP**

partner's name

STUDENT A Work with a partner. One of you works on this page. The other works on page 6. Don't look at your partner's page.

With your partner, match each CD with a music review (description).

Part One

Below you'll find the covers for three CDs. Your partner has reviews of each of these CDs. Listen to your partner read the reviews. Decide which musicians and CD titles go with which CD covers. Ask your partner to repeat information if necessary. Write your answers below.

Name of Musician/Band   **Name of Musician/Band**   **Name of Musician/Band**

_____   _____   _____

Title of CD   **Title of CD**   **Title of CD**

_____   _____   _____

Part Two

Below you'll find the reviews of the CDs on page 6. Read them to your partner. Repeat any information if necessary. Help him/her match the reviews to the CD covers and write the names.

1. Mary Douglas's new CD, *Guitar Songs*, is fantastic! The variety of songs on this CD shows her great singing and song-writing talent. The song "New York Blues" is sure to be a hit!

2. Thomas Long plays rock saxophone at its best on his new CD, *All Night Long*. Most of the songs were written by Thomas, but there also are two jazz classics.

3. In her new CD, *Close Up*, Jane Collins sings about the sad side of life. By the end of the CD, I was tired of hearing about her bad relationships and disappointments. I don't recommend this one.

INFORMATION GAP Rock and Roll Music

8 | **PARTNER** | **INFORMATION GAP**

STUDENT B Work with a partner. One of you works on this page. The other works on page 5. Don't look at your partner's page.

With your partner, match each music review (description) with a CD.

Part One

Below you'll find the reviews of the CDs on page 5. Read them to your partner. Repeat any information if necessary. Help him/her match the reviews to the CDs and write the names.

1. The Good Notes, an all-female group, has a new CD called *Where Are We Now?* These women know rock and roll! I danced to all of the songs! I especially liked "Don't Listen." It has a fantastic piano solo by María Ricardo.

2. *Drum Head* is the first CD by the Boston hard rock group the Monsters. Their music is loud and angry. If that's what you like, you'll love this one!

3. The Blue Boys have a new CD, *Back to the Past*, and that's exactly where it takes you. They play rock versions of well-known songs, using traditional instruments like the fiddle, bass, banjo, and guitar.

Part Two

Below you'll the covers for three CDs. Your partner has reviews of each of the CDs. Listen to your partner read the reviews. Decide which musicians and CD titles go with which CD covers. Ask your partner to repeat information if necessary. Write your answers below.

Name of Musician/Band

_____

Title of CD

_____

Name of Musician/Band

_____

Title of CD

_____

Name of Musician/Band

_____

Title of CD

_____

Unexpected Offers

EPISODE **41**

THEMES
- Moving to a Different Country
- Invitations
- The Christmas Spirit

GAME
- Giving Christmas Presents

OPTIONAL PROJECT
- Vacations (Appendix 5)

THEME ## Moving to a Different Country

---

1 **GROUP** **BRAINSTORM**

_____
group number

In this episode, Mr. and Mrs. Wang talk about moving to Taiwan.

When people move to a different country, what do they have to adjust to? With your group, make a list. The first two are done for you.

When you move to a different country,...

1. sometimes you have to learn a new language.
2. the food is usually different.
3. _____
4. _____
5. _____
6. _____
7. _____
8. _____

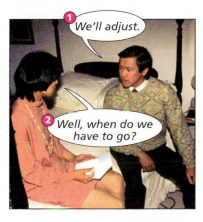

We'll adjust.

Well, when do we have to go?

---

2 **PARTNER** **INTERVIEW**

_____
partner's name

A. Work with a partner from your group in Activity 1. Which three items in Activity 1 do you think are most difficult to adjust to? Circle your answers in the box below.

B. Find out what your partner thinks. Say: _You move to a different country. What three things are most difficult to adjust to?_ Circle your partner's answers. Are your answers similar?

You			
1	2	3	4
5	6	7	8

Your partner			
1	2	3	4
5	6	7	8

THEME Invitations

Ramón invites Rebecca to go with him to the community center on Christmas.
Here are some ways that people extend invitations:

partner's name

Would you consider spending Christmas with me?

Would you care to dance?	**How about** getting a cup of coffee?
Would you like to go out for dinner?	**Would you consider** going to the party with me?

Here are some ways to accept or refuse invitations:

Ways to accept an invitation:	*Ways to refuse an invitation:*
I'd like that.	Thank you, but no.
That would be very nice.	I'm afraid I can't. Maybe another time.
Sure, sounds great.	Thank you, but I have to _____.

Work with a partner. Look at the situations below. Take turns. One person chooses a situation and extends an invitation. The other person accepts or refuses the invitation. Then, make up your own situation.

EXAMPLE   Student A: Would you like to come to the cafeteria with us?   Student B: Thank you, but I have to study.

Invite your partner to do the following:

1. study together

   Student A _____

   Student B _____

2. practice speaking English

   Student A _____

   Student B _____

3. go to a movie

   Student A _____

   Student B _____

4. get something to drink in a café

   Student A _____

   Student B _____

5. Your situation: _____

   Student A _____

   Student B _____

 *What About YOU?*

1. What was the last thing you invited somebody to do?
2. When was the last time you received an invitation?
3. Do you ever get invitations to events that you don't want to go to? If so, do you usually accept or refuse the invitation?

a.

Dr. and Mrs. John Baker
request the pleasure of your
company
at the marriage of their
daughter
Kathleen Louise
to Mr. Alfred Jackson
on June 20
at four o'clock
at St. John's Episcopal
Church
Springfield, Connecticut

Reception at Young Manor.
RSVP on enclosed card.

b.

Hey grads—

WE DID IT!
LET'S PARTY!

Campus Center Ballroom
Friday, May 25
from 9:00 to whenever
Music by DJ Stan the Man
Campus Center snack bar
open till midnight

c.

It's a baby shower for
Jessica
Given by
Ann and Deborah
To be held at
Ann's—98 Bridge Rd., Apt. 224
on Sunday the 12th at 7:00
RSVP Deb 555-8741 (home)
or 555-4200 (work)

d.

You're invited to a
birthday party!
For: DANNY
On: Saturday, Oct. 15
From: 2:00   To: 4:00
At: 24 East Park Street
RSVP by: Monday, October 10
Phone: 555-8933

e.

Luis—
There's a cookout
at Jones's beach on
Friday after school.
Please come. Call me
if you need directions.
Rosa

f.

Come to a goodbye party!
For: Marilyn and Richard Sims
On: Friday, April 25
From: 7:00   To: 10:00
At: The Clarks' House
4515 North Ashland

A. With your partner, match the invitations and the events. Write the letter of the invitation next to the event below.

B. Check (✔) the invitations to which you should R.S.V.P. (R.S.V.P. means to answer the invitation—to write or call to say whether or not you can go.)

                               RSVP?   RSVP?

_____ **1.** a birthday party   _____   _____ **4.** a wedding   _____

_____ **2.** a graduation party   _____   _____ **5.** a beach party   _____

_____ **3.** a party for a woman   _____   _____ **6.** a party for someone   _____
        who is having a baby   who is moving

1. Which of the parties above would you like to go to?
2. When do people in your country send written invitations?
3. When was the last time you sent a written invitation?
     What was the invitation?

THEME The Christmas Spirit

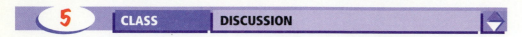

5   **CLASS**   **DISCUSSION**

In this episode, Ramón talks about bringing food to the community center for Christmas. Rebecca tells him that he has the true Christmas spirit. The expression "having the Christmas spirit" means honoring Christmas traditions. It means giving to others, both the ones you love and strangers in need.

On what other holidays do people show a spirit of giving? Discuss this as a class. Your teacher will complete a chart like the following on the board.

What is the holiday?	Who celebrates it?	How do people show the spirit of giving?
1. Christmas	Christians	In the U.S. and Canada, families and friends give gifts. People give money to the poor. People serve Christmas dinners in community centers.
2.		
3.		

6   **GROUP**   **PRESENTATION**

_____
group number

At Christmas time, people give money to charities. Charities help people in different ways. But all charities need money to give help. You're going to try to help a charity raise some money.

Preparation

A. Divide into groups. Each group chooses a different kind of charity. Groups can choose from the charities below, or they can think of their own.

shelter for people without homes	shelter for battered women
community center that gives food to the poor	group that gives scholarships to music students
group that helps people in retirement homes	group that gives sports equipment to poor children

B. In your groups, think of reasons why people would give money to your charity. Make a list of all the good things the charity does.

C. Each group will make a presentation to the class. The group members will tell the class about the good things the charity does, and try to persuade the class to give money to the charity. Your group will only have three minutes to make your presentation.

Presentation

A. Each student in the class has $100 to give to the charities. You can't give the money to your own group's charity. Listen to the presentations, and decide how to spend your money.

B. On a piece of paper, write (1) the charities you want to give money to and (2) the amount of money for each charity. Give your paper to your teacher. Your teacher will tell the class which charities collected the most money.

GAME **Giving Christmas Presents**

7 **PARTNER** **GAME**

_____
partner's name

It's Christmas. Many people in the United States give presents to friends and family members. The Sills, Chills, Bills, and Tills families exchange presents at Christmas every year. They put the presents under the tree. But this year the Chills baby pulled the name tags off the presents. The Chills now have to match the presents to the people. You will help them. Work with a partner. The winner is the _first pair_ to match the presents correctly.

Play the Game

- Look at the presents on this page. Look at the people on page 6.
- When your teacher tells you, read the clues on Appendix 13 at the back of the book.
- Try to find the pattern: _Why do certain people get certain gifts?_ Remember, you have to think fast! Hint: You will need to count!
- Write the name of the present for each person in the blanks on page 6.
- When you finish, raise your hand. Your teacher will check your answers.
- A pair wins if all the answers are correct. But the pair is out of the game if all the answers aren't correct. The game continues with the other pairs.

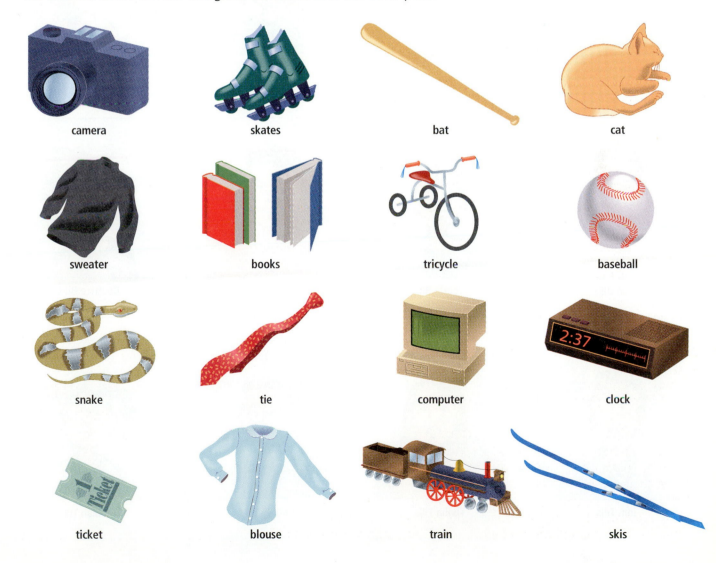

camera	skates	bat	cat
sweater	books	tricycle	baseball
snake	tie	computer	clock
ticket	blouse	train	skis

Saul Sills

Susanna Sills

Sally Sills

Samuel Sills

Carson Chills

Cindy Chills

Caroline Chills

Cal Chills

Brian Bills

Brenda Bills

Ben Bills

Beatrice Bills

Tom Tills

Thalia Tills

Teddy Tills

Tallulah Tills

The Audition

EPISODE **42**

THEMES
- Waiting
- The Importance of Education
- An Audition

SONG
- Dream Catcher

OPTIONAL PROJECT
- Dedication (Appendix 6)

THEME **Waiting**

---

1 | CLASS | BRAINSTORM

In this episode, Rebecca and Bill have to wait a long time for an audition. As a class, think of a list of eight common situations in which people wait. Use the pictures to get some ideas. Write your list below the pictures. (You will use the boxes in Activity 2.)

...Please wait... ...someone will be with you shortly...

1. _____ ☐   5. _____ ☐
2. _____ ☐   6. _____ ☐
3. _____ ☐   7. _____ ☐
4. _____ ☐   8. _____ ☐

---

2 | GROUP | SURVEY

_____
group number

Find out when the members of your group hate to wait the most.

A. Divide into groups. Look at the list of situations from Activity 1.

B. Ask this question: *When do you really hate to wait?* Each person can vote for only three situations. Count the votes for each situation and write the number in the boxes in Activity 1.

C. Compare your group's answers with those of other groups. Are the answers alike? When do your classmates really hate to wait?

partner's name

How long would you wait for certain things? Write the times in the chart. Then, ask your partner the questions and write his/her times.

	TIME	
How long would you wait. . .	**You**	**Your partner**
to get a table in a restaurant?		
to buy a ticket for a concert?		
to buy something on sale?		
for a job interview?		
for an appointment with a friend?		
for an appointment with a doctor?		

4 CLASS DATA ANALYSIS

As a class, tell the teacher your times from Activity 3. The teacher will write the numbers on the board. Find the average waiting time for the class for each item. Then, answer these questions:

■ *For how many items are you above the class average?* _____

■ *For how many items are you below the class average?* _____

As a class, discuss this question: *Are you surprised by how long people wait for things?*

THEME The Importance of Education

5 CLASS DISCUSSION

School is very important to Rebecca. How important do *you* think school is? Read the following sentences. Check (✔) *I agree* or *I disagree*. Discuss your answers with the class.

I've got to focus on school.

	I agree	disagree
1. Education is necessary to be successful.		
2. Education is helpful to be successful.		
3. Education doesn't help people be successful.		
4. You have to go to an expensive school to get a good education.		
5. You have to go to school to get an education.		
6. It's possible to have too much education.		

Parents and their children sometimes have very different views on education. Many times parents want their children to get an education, while the children don't always want to continue their studies.

A. Divide into groups of three. One person should take the role of the child, and the other two will be the parents. Take the following positions:

> **Child:** _You just want to get a job. You're not interested in studying more right now. You don't know what you want to be. You want to learn about the world before you decide on a career. Persuade your parents that you're doing what's right for you._

> **Parents:** _Money for college tuition is no problem for you. You want your child to go to school so he/she can get the best job possible. Persuade your child to go to college._

B. When you're finished, discuss your role-play. What happened?

7 **GROUP**   **PRESENTATION**

_____
group number

Imagine that you're in a country where English is not the first language. You're on a parent committee at your local school. The school has to decide whether or not to offer English classes to children. Your group will make a presentation to support English classes.

A. Divide into groups. Discuss this question: _Why is it important for people to learn English?_ Make a list of reasons. Be ready to explain each one.

Reasons to learn English

_____   _____
_____   _____
_____   _____
_____   _____
_____   _____

B. Take turns. Each group has five minutes to present its ideas.

C. As a class, discuss the best reasons you heard in the presentations.

1. Would you like to have more education?
2. What would you like to study?
3. Why are _you_ studying English?

THEME An Audition

8   CLASS   GAME

In this episode, Bill and Rebecca go on an audition. Now it's your turn. You are auditioning for a part in the *Connect with English* video.

A. Work with a partner. Choose a scene from *Connect with English* program. You will use the scene for your audition. It can be any scene from the series. Choose the character that each of you will play. Write the scene and the characters on a piece of paper. Don't show your paper to your classmates.

EXAMPLE

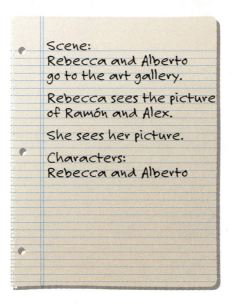

Scene:
Rebecca and Alberto go to the art gallery.

Rebecca sees the picture of Ramón and Alex.

She sees her picture.

Characters:
Rebecca and Alberto

B. With your partner, prepare a script. You don't need to use the exact words from the video, but you should present the general ideas. Also, think about the gestures and body language you will use. Your scene will need to be one minute long.

C. Rehearse your scene.

The Game
- Give your paper to your teacher.
- Each pair acts out its scene for the class.
- The other pairs will try to guess the characters and the scene. On a piece of paper, they write down their guesses. After all the auditions, they give their paper to the teacher to score.

Scoring
This is how pairs can earn points:
- Each pair gets one point for each correct scene and characters it names.
- Each pair also gets one point for every pair in the class that correctly guesses its scene.

The pair with the most points wins!

1. Have you ever had an audition?
2. If yes, what was it for?
3. Do you get nervous before auditions or interviews?

SONG **Dream Catcher**

9	PARTNER	SONG	

_____

partner's name

In this episode, Rebecca sings her song, "Dream Catcher."
With your group, look at the words of the song and discuss them.
Answer the questions below.

1 All the lights are shining bright down in the city,

2 Shining like a million dreams.

3 Sometimes I feel like I'm upside down—

4 All those dreams are falling right past me.

5 Everybody needs a dream catcher,

6 Someone to be there when your dreams start to fall.

7 Everybody needs a dream catcher,

8 Someone to be there when the bad dreams are all you can see.

9 Dream catcher, catch me.

Dream catcher, catch me.

Circle your answers:

1. How does the singer of this song feel?

   a. happy   **b.** sad   **c.** angry

2. What are the "dreams" in Rebecca's song?

   a. good dreams at night   **b.** bad dreams during the day   **c.** hopes

3. In line 4 the singer says, "All those dreams are falling right past me."
   What does this mean?

   a. The singer has too many dreams.   **b.** The singer is losing her dreams.

4. In Rebecca's song, what is a dream catcher?

   a. a thing   **b.** an idea   **c.** a person

Write your answers:

5. What does the singer want the dream catcher to catch? _____

   _____

6. How can someone be a dream catcher? _____

   _____

Compare answers with another pair. Discuss the reasons for your answers.

S O N G **Dream Catcher**

10   **GROUP**   **DRAWING**

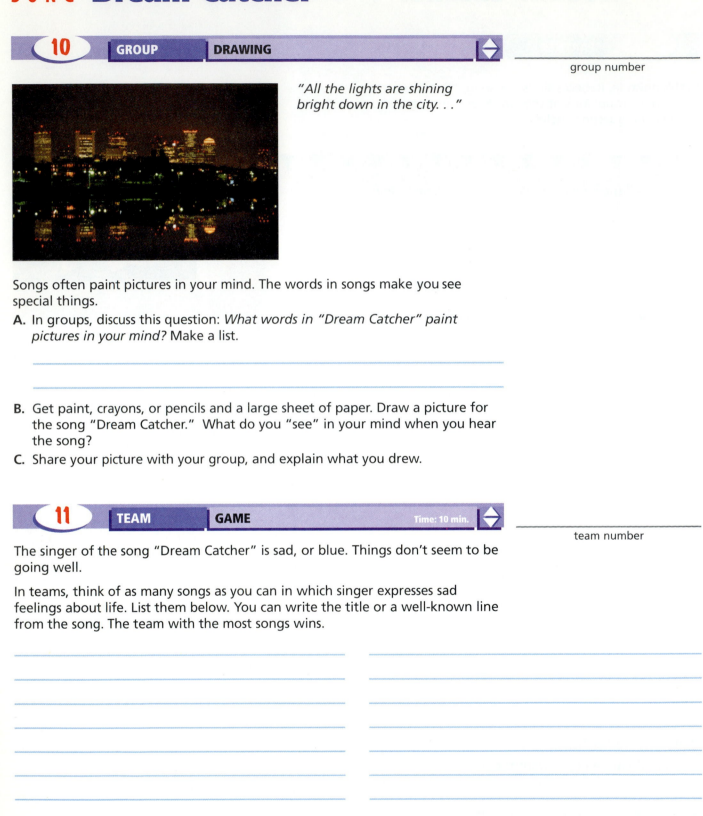

*"All the lights are shining
bright down in the city. . ."*

Songs often paint pictures in your mind. The words in songs make you see
special things.

A. In groups, discuss this question: *What words in "Dream Catcher" paint
pictures in your mind?* Make a list.

_____

_____

B. Get paint, crayons, or pencils and a large sheet of paper. Draw a picture for
the song "Dream Catcher." What do you "see" in your mind when you hear
the song?

C. Share your picture with your group, and explain what you drew.

11   **TEAM**   **GAME**   **Time: 10 min.**

The singer of the song "Dream Catcher" is sad, or blue. Things don't seem to be
going well.

In teams, think of as many songs as you can in which singer expresses sad
feelings about life. List them below. You can write the title or a well-known line
from the song. The team with the most songs wins.

Dream Catcher

THEMES
- Success
- Talent
- Having Confidence

INFORMATION GAP
- Taking a Message

OPTIONAL PROJECT
- Chocolates (Appendix 7)

T H E M E Success

| **1** | **PARTNER** | **RANKING** |

partner's name

In this episode, Bill talks about success. What does "success" mean to you?

A. Look at the statements in the chart below. Decide how important each item is to your idea of success. Circle your answers.

B. Find out what your partner thinks. Ask this question: *How important is making a lot of money*? Circle your partner's answers.

> *Being a success in the music business means more than just making music. It means making money.*

```
1 = Very important
2 = Important
3 = Somewhat important
4 = Not very important
5 = Not important at all
```

How important is ...	You	Your partner
making a lot of money?	1 2 3 4 5	1 2 3 4 5
being famous?	1 2 3 4 5	1 2 3 4 5
living in a big house?	1 2 3 4 5	1 2 3 4 5
having an important job?	1 2 3 4 5	1 2 3 4 5
being the best at what you do?	1 2 3 4 5	1 2 3 4 5
being free to do what you like?	1 2 3 4 5	1 2 3 4 5
having a nice family?	1 2 3 4 5	1 2 3 4 5
having an expensive car?	1 2 3 4 5	1 2 3 4 5

What About YOU?

1. Is anyone you know successful?
2. In what way is this person a success?

3. What do you think are the reasons for his or her success?
4. Would you like to have this same kind of success?

2   CLASS   BINGO

Who in your class has talent? Look at the squares below. You're going to try to find people with these talents.

A. Take your book and a pencil. Move around the class, and ask questions. For example, ask:
  ■ *Are you a good singer?*
  ■ *Can you swim?*

B. When someone says "Yes," write the person's name on the line in that square. When someone says "No," ask another question. Or you can ask someone else the same question.

C. To win, get five *different* names in a row (across, up and down, or diagonally). When you have five names, say "Bingo! "The first person to say "Bingo" is the winner.

D. The winner will do the following: Tell the class the five people and what talents they have.

_____ is a good singer.	_____ can draw.	_____ can whistle.	_____ can do gymnastics.	_____ is a good actor.
_____ can play a musical instrument.	_____ is good at math.	_____ can ride a horse.	_____ can speak languages.	_____ can tell jokes.
_____ can roller-skate.	_____ can wiggle his or her ears.	**FREE**	_____ is a good cook.	_____ can swim.
_____ can sew.	_____ can ride a bike.	_____ can repair a car.	_____ can take good pictures.	_____ can sail a boat.
_____ can do magic tricks.	_____ is good at a sport.	_____ can write computer programs.	_____ is a good dancer.	_____ can tell stories.

What About YOU?

1. What's your best talent?
2. What talent would you like to have?
3. Is talent something a person is born with?

The year is 2039. The earth is in trouble. A giant comet is going to hit the earth soon. Everyone is trying to escape to other planets.

There is room on a spaceship for one more person. The group needs a person with valuable talents.

A. You want to go on the spaceship. Try to persuade the group to take you along. On a separate piece of paper, write a list of your talents. Use the information in the box below for help.

Useful expressions:	Questions the group may ask you:
I can <u>speak two languages</u>.	Can you <u>use a computer</u>?
I am <u>strong and healthy</u>.	Are you <u>intelligent</u>?
I'm good at <u>working with others</u>.	Are you good at <u>fixing things</u>?
I'm a good <u>cook</u>.	Are you a good <u>worker</u>?
I know how to <u>fly a spaceship</u>.	Do you know how to <u>farm</u>?

B. Present your information to the group. Be ready to answer any of their questions. The group will take notes on your presentation.

C. After the presentations, talk about the most useful talents each person has. Who should be the person to get the last spot on the spaceship?

THEME Having Confidence

In this episode, Bill talks about his future in music. He is very confident. He also has confidence in Rebecca. Musicians need confidence to perform in front of people. Who else needs confidence?

With your group, complete the sentences below about people who need confidence. Be sure to explain why these people need confidence.

EXAMPLE   ___Musicians___ need confidence because ___they perform in front of people___ .

1. _____ need/s confidence because _____ .

2. _____ need/s confidence because _____ .

3. _____ need/s confidence because _____ .

4. _____ need/s confidence because _____ .

5. _____ need/s confidence because _____ .

A. Read the statements below about confidence. Are they true or false? Check (✔) your answers.

B. Divide into groups of three. How do the people in your group feel about confidence? Listen to your group members and write their answers in the chart. Ask them to explain any answers that you don't understand.

	You		Group member 1		Group member 2	
	True	False	True	False	True	False
1. Confidence is an important quality.						
2. It's better to have too little confidence than too much.						
3. Confidence helps people to succeed.						
4. Confidence comes after you are successful.						
5. Men usually have more confidence than women.						

Divide into teams. With your teammates, think of words or names from the *Connect with English* story that start with each of the letters below. The team with the most words wins.

C	O	N	F	I	D	E	N	T
college	opera tickets	Nancy						

What About YOU?

1. Are you usually a confident person?
2. In what situations do you feel most confident?
3. In what situations would you like to have more confidence?

INFORMATION GAP Taking a Message

STUDENT A Work with a partner. One of you works on this page. The other works on page 6. Don't look at your partner's page.

Part One

You're going to call a friend. Your partner will answer the phone. Your friend isn't home, so you have to leave a message.

A. Choose a name for your friend. On the phone, you'll ask to speak to him or her. Here are some ways people ask for someone on the phone:

Hello. May I please speak to _____?

   or

Hello. This is _____ . Is _____ there?

B. Choose one of the situations below and leave this message for your friend.

> 1. *You and your friend plan to see a movie. It starts at 8:00 p.m. You want him/her to meet you at 7:45 in front of the Central Square Cinema.*

> 2. *You want to invite your friend to a concert. It's next Saturday. You want your friend to call you back as soon as possible because you need to buy tickets.*

> 3. *You want your friend to pick you up at the airport. Your flight arrives next Sunday at 7:50 p.m. It's World Air flight number 2047.*

Part Two

Change roles with your partner. You'll answer the phone. Your partner's friend isn't there. You will offer to take a message.

A. Here are some ways people offer to take messages:

> Would you like to leave a message?
>
>   **or**
>
> Can I give him/her a message?

B. Use the form at the right to write down the message.

Part Three

Show your partner the message you took in Part Two. Is it correct?

To: _____

Date: _____ Time: _____

WHILE YOU WERE OUT

Name _____

Phone _____

Message _____

_____

_____

_____

_____

INFORMATION GAP Taking a Message

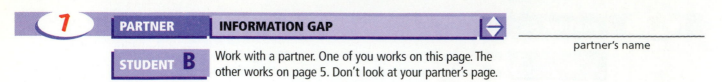

STUDENT B Work with a partner. One of you works on this page. The other works on page 5. Don't look at your partner's page.

Part One

Your partner is going to call a friend. You answer the phone. The friend isn't there. You'll need to take a message.

A. Answer the phone. Offer to take a message. Here are some ways people offer to take messages:

> Would you like to leave a message?
>
> **or**
>
> Can I give him/her a message?

B. Use the form at the right to write down the message.

To: _____

Date: _____ Time: _____

WHILE YOU WERE OUT

Name _____

Phone _____

Message _____

_____

_____

_____

_____

Part Two

Change roles with your partner. Now you'll call a friend. Choose a name for your friend.

A. Here are some ways people ask for someone on the phone:

> Hello. May I please speak to _____?
>
> **or**
>
> Hello. This is _____ . Is _____ there?

B. Choose one of the situations below and leave this message for your friend.

> 1. *You and your friend talked about going out for dinner tonight. You want to meet at Café Brasilia at 7:15.*

> 2. *You want to invite your friend to a soccer game. It's next Sunday. Your friend should call you back as soon as possible.*

> 3. *Your friend wants to buy a bicycle. There's a big sale tomorrow at Bicycle World. It starts at 9:30 a.m.*

Part Three

Show your partner the message you took in Part One. Is it correct?

Gifts

EPISODE 44

THEMES
- The Community Center
- Breaking Up
- Inspirations

GAME
- Skiing

OPTIONAL PROJECT
- Helping People in the Community (Appendix 8)

THEME The Community Center

1 GROUP   DISCUSSION

_____
group number

In this episode, Ramón and Rebecca take food to the community center for Christmas dinner. A community center helps people in many ways.

A. You and the members of your group run a community center. Your center usually helps the community in all of the ways below. Add one more activity to the list below.

B. This year, the center doesn't have enough money to do everything. With your group, choose six of the items below for the center to do. Check (✔) your answers.

_____ give food to poor people

_____ take care of children whose parents work

_____ take care of older people who don't have anyone to help them

_____ give free medical care to poor people

_____ teach job skills and adult education classes

_____ give homeless people a place to sleep

_____ help people keep their neighborhood safe and clean

_____ hold religious services

_____ organize sports teams for neighborhood children

_____ your own idea: _____

2 CLASS   POLL

Which items from the list in Activity 1 were the most popular?

A. Your teacher will copy the list from Activity 1 onto the board.

B. As your teacher reads each item, have a group leader raise his or her hand if your group checked that item.

C. Count the number of groups that put a ✔ next to each item. Your teacher will write this number on the board next to each item.

D. What were the six most popular answers?

Ramón brings food to people at the community center on Christmas. Many community centers also deliver food to people in their homes. Often the people are elderly or are too sick to leave their house.

Work with your partner. You have to deliver meals to five people in an apartment building, but the meals and the apartment numbers are mixed up. Read the clues. Match the meal to the right person. Write the letter of each meal on the correct floor.

Some of the people in the building have these special food requirements:
- One person is a vegetarian. He doesn't eat meat.
- One person can't eat sweets or cakes.
- One person won't eat beef.
- One person can't have milk products like cheese or ice cream.

The Meals
A. pizza with cheese and tomato, salad, lemonade
B. chicken, beans, cake, and coffee
C. chicken, beans, corn, tea
D. hamburger, fries, ice cream, soda
E. hamburger, fries, apple, tea

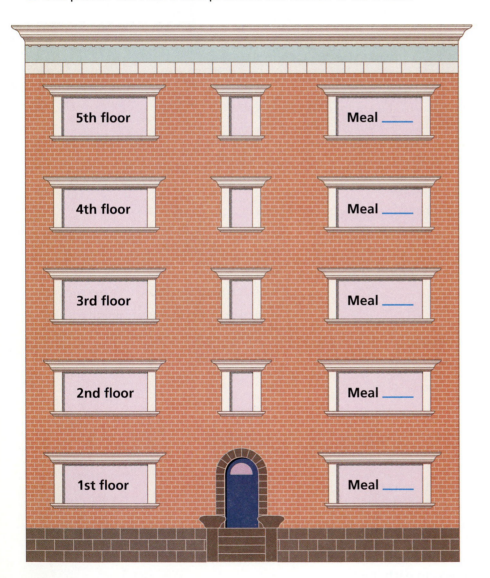

5th floor　　Meal _____

4th floor　　Meal _____

3rd floor　　Meal _____

2nd floor　　Meal _____

1st floor　　Meal _____

C L U E S

► The vegetarian lives above the person who can't eat sweets. He lives below the person who can't have milk products.

► The person who can't eat milk products wants beef.

► The person who can't eat beef lives on the first floor.

► The person who can't eat milk products lives on the top floor.

What About YOU?

1. Is there a community center close to your neighborhood? If so, where is it?
2. What services does the center offer?
3. Have you ever been to a community center? If so, what did you do there?

Breaking Up

4 | **GROUP** | **OPINION SURVEY**

_____
group number

In this episode, Alberto tells Rebecca that he just wants to be friends. When people break up, they often want to stay friends.

A. Circle your answers to the questions in the chart below.

B. Divide into groups. Find out how many people in your group believe it's possible to be friends after a breakup. Ask these questions:
- *Can people be friends after they break up?*
- *Is it easy for people to be friends after they break up?*

C. Circle your group members' answers.

Name	Sex (M/F)	Can people be friends after they break up?		Is it easy for people to be friends after they break up?	
You		Yes	No	Yes	No
1.		Yes	No	Yes	No
2.		Yes	No	Yes	No
3.		Yes	No	Yes	No
4.		Yes	No	Yes	No

5 | **PARTNER** | **DATA ANALYSIS**

_____
partner's name

Work with a partner from a different group. Compare surveys from Activity 4.

1. What is the total number of *women* who answered the questions? _____

What is the total number of *men* who answered the questions? _____

2. How many *women* thought people could be friends after a breakup? _____

How many *men* thought people could be friends after a breakup? _____

Who answered "Yes" to this question more often—women or men? _____

3. How many *women* thought it was easy to be friends after a breakup? _____

How many *men* thought it was easy to be friends after a breakup? _____

Who answered "Yes" to this question more often—women or men? _____

What About YOU?

1. Have you ever broken up with someone?
2. If so, are you still friends with that person?
3. Do you know any people who are still friends after a breakup?
4. Why do people want to stay friends after a breakup?

THEME Inspirations

_____
partner's name

Alberto gave Rebecca a dream catcher. Rebecca told him that the dream catcher inspired her to write her song. It gave her the idea, or the *inspiration* for the song.

Inspirations can come from either people or things. For example, a good teacher might inspire you to read a book, or study a certain subject. A beautiful photograph of an island might inspire you to visit that place for a vacation.

Did a person or a thing ever "inspire" *you* to do something?

Step One

Ask your partner the questions below. They're about an inspiration. Write what your partner says.

1. What was your inspiration? Was it a person or a thing? _____

   _____

2. What did the person or thing do to inspire you? _____

3. Why was this special? _____

4. What did you do because of this inspiration? _____

5. How do you feel about this inspiration now? _____

6. Your own question: _____

Step Two

Write a short paragraph below about the inspiration that your partner described.

_____
_____
_____
_____
_____
_____
_____
_____
_____
_____
_____
_____
_____
_____
_____

Step Three

When you're done writing, read what you have written to your partner.
Your partner will tell you if you have understood everything correctly.

G A M E Skiing

7 **TEAM** **GAME**

Play this game and go skiing with Alberto. The team that hits the fewest trees wins!

Get Ready to Play

Step One
Divide into an even number of teams. The teacher will number the teams. Team 1 will play Team 2, Team 3 will play Team 4, and so on.

Step Two
With your teammates, think of five words from the *Connect with English* video. Write them below. They can be words for people, places, or things. They should be words you have discussed in class. Don't show the words to the other team.

***Connect with English* words:**

EXAMPLE ____goggles____

1. _____ 2. _____ 3. _____ 4. _____ 5. _____

Step Three
One player from each team cuts out the trees on Appendix 13. Each team will cut out and use the game board on page 6. Now you're ready to play.

Play the Game
- On a piece of paper or the board, the other team will write spaces for each letter of their first word.

  EXAMPLE For goggles, they would write: ___ ___ ___ ___ ___ ___ ___

- Try to guess the letters in the other team's word.
- If you guess a letter that *isn't* in the word, put a tree in front of your skier on your team's gameboard. Then, guess another letter.
- If your team guesses a letter that *is* in the word, the other team will write the letter in the correct space (or spaces).

  EXAMPLE For goggles, if you guess the letter E, they will write:
  ___ ___ ___ ___ ___ E ___

- Continue to guess letters. When you know the whole word, guess it!
- If your team guesses the wrong word, put TWO trees in front of your skier. You can continue to guess letters or words.
- If you guess the correct word, your turn is finished. Don't remove your trees from the gameboard yet!
- Change roles. Now, the other team tries to guess one of your words. Your team will write the spaces for the letters that the other team will guess.
- After each team has had a turn at guessing a word, count the number of trees in front each team's skier. The team with the fewest trees wins the round. Record the winner in the chart on page 6. Remove the trees and play another round. Play five rounds in all.

GAME Skiing

Which team won the most rounds?

Round 1 _____

Round 2 _____

Round 3 _____

Round 4 _____

Round 5 _____

True Love

THEMES
- An Ekeko
- Exchanging Christmas Presents
- Falling in Love

INFORMATION GAP
- Planning a Trip

OPTIONAL PROJECT
- Legends (Appendix 9)

THEME **An Ekeko**

| 1 | PARTNER | INTERVIEW |

partner's name

In this episode, Ramón gives Rebecca an ekeko. According to an old Peruvian legend, if you hang your dreams on the ekeko, they will come true. Ramón hangs an item on the ekeko for each of Rebecca's dreams.

A. Now it's your turn. Work with a partner. What three items would you put on *your* ekeko? You can choose any of the items below, or you can think of others. In the chart, write the names of the items and what they mean to you.

B. Then, interview your partner. Ask your partner these questions:
- *What items would you put on your ekeko?*
- *Why would you put a diploma on the ekeko? What does it mean to you?*

Write your partner's answers.

a diploma   a ring   a passport   a pen   a star   a heart

	Your item	What it means	Your partner's item	What it means
EXAMPLE	a gold record	having a hit song	a ring	marriage
1.				
2.				
3.				

Play a guessing game with ekeko items.

A. Write your ekeko items from Activity 1 on a small piece of paper. Write your name on it and give it to your teacher. Don't show it to anyone else!

EXAMPLE

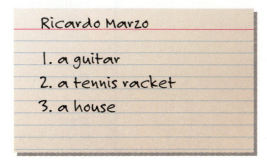

Ricardo Marzo

1. a guitar
2. a tennis racket
3. a house

B. Divide into two teams. Your partner from Activity 1 can't be on your team.

C. Team 1 sends two players to the board. One student faces the board (*Student A*), the other student faces away from it (*Student B*).

D. The teacher will choose one of your classmates' papers and will write the three ekeko items on the board. *Student A* will try to explain the items on the board to *Student B*. *Student B* will try to guess the items. *Student A* and *Student B* have two minutes to explain and guess all three items. The team gets one point for each correct answer.

E. The teams take turns sending pairs to the board. The game is over when all students on both teams have had a turn at the board. The team with the most points wins.

 **3**   **CLASS**   **DISCUSSION**

As a class, discuss the ekeko items. Each person tells the class what her/his items are and what they mean. Then, answer the following questions:

- *What was the most common ekeko item in the class?*
- *What were the most unusual ekeko items in the class?*
- *Did any two people have the same three ekeko items?*

T H E M E Exchanging Christmas Presents

4 PARTNER **WAYS TO SAY IT**   _____

partner's name

In this episode, Rebecca and Ramón exchange Christmas presents. They're very happy with their gifts. Here are some ways to say you like a present in English:

I love it!	It's just what I wanted!	Oh, it's great/awesome!
Wow! Thank you so much!	It's just what I needed!	What a beautiful shirt!

Work with a partner. Look at the situations below. Take turns. One person chooses a situation. The other person chooses an expression from above. Then, make up your own situation.

	Situations	Expressions
EXAMPLE	Your mother gives you a warm jacket.	Thanks, Mom! It's just what I needed!
1.	Your girlfriend/boyfriend gives you a ring.	_____
2.	Your grandfather gives you a watch.	_____
3.	Your parents give you a new car.	_____
4.	Your situation:	_____

5 GROUP **DISCUSSION**   _____

group number

A. Divide into three groups. With your group members, you'll talk about classmates who *are not in your group*. For example, Group 1 talks about Group 2, Group 2 talks about Group 3, and Group 3 talks about Group 1.

B. For each person in the other group, discuss this question: *What are his/her likes and interests?*

C. Decide on a gift for each person. You want the present to be the best gift the person has ever received!

EXAMPLE   The person really likes music.

Gift: The latest CD in the music style the person likes best

D. Write your gift decision for each person on a piece of paper and give it to the person.

E. As a class, discuss the gifts that each person received. Were people surprised with their gift? Were most people happy with the gift?

THEME Falling in Love

6 **PARTNER** **DISCUSSION**

partner's name

good looks	nice family	intelligence	money
kindness	talent	humor	fame
interest in children	dedication	same religion	sense of responsibility

Work with a partner. Discuss why Ramón and Rebecca are falling in love.

A. From the list above, choose the two most important reasons that Ramón is falling in love with Rebecca. Write them below.

Why Ramón is falling in love with Rebecca

1. _____

2. _____

B. From the list above, choose the two most important reasons that Rebecca is falling in love with Ramón. Write them below.

Why Rebecca is falling in love with Ramón

1. _____

2. _____

7 **GROUP** **DISCUSSION**

group number

A. Look again at the list of reasons in Activity 6. With the members of your group, answer these questions:
- *Which do you think are the three "best" reasons for falling in love?*
- *Which do you think are the three "worst" reasons for falling in love?*

B. Complete the chart.

Best reasons for falling in love	Worst reasons for falling in love
1.	1.
2.	2.
3.	3.

C. Share your answers with the class. Are there any reasons that every group listed? What are they?

1. Do people think of reasons when they fall in love?
2. What is "love at first sight"?
3. Do you think "love at first sight" is possible?
4. How do you know when you're in love?

INFORMATION GAP Planning a Trip

8	**PARTNER**	**INFORMATION GAP**	

STUDENT A — Work with a partner. One of you works on this page. The other works on page 6. Don't look at your partner's page.

partner's name

Part One

In this episode, Kevin begins planning for his trip to San Francisco. Now it's your turn to plan a trip! Talk to a travel agent. Find out the best tour for you.

Boston

You want to take a tour of Boston and the eastern part of the United States. You're interested in visiting museums and historical places. You don't want to spend more than $1,500 for the tour. You want to stay one week. Your partner is a travel agent. He/she has some tours to sell. Ask questions about the tours. Decide which one is best for you. Write its number in the space below.

Ask questions like these:
- *What places does the tour go to?*
- *What things do you do with the tour group?*
- *How long is the tour?*
- *How much does the tour cost? What is included in the cost?*

Number of the tour you will take: _____

Part Two

Read the information on these three tours to the western part of the United States. Your partner will ask you questions about the tours. Help him/her find the best tour.

1. **West Coast Adventure Tour**
   You'll go skiing in the Rocky Mountains. You'll go down the fast-moving waters of the Colorado River on a raft. You'll climb mountains in California. These are just three of the adventures you will have on this tour. You will also stay in the best hotels. The tour is for eight days. Hotel and meals are included in the price of $2,500.

2. **Western Cities Tour**
   See the cities in the western part of the United States. This tour takes you to Los Angeles, San Francisco, and Seattle. Visit the movie studios in Hollywood. See Chinatown in San Francisco. Drive through the redwood forests of Northern California. Go to the top of the Space Needle in Seattle. You'll see all the main sights of the West Coast cities. You will stay in good quality hotels. The tour is for seven days. The price includes hotel costs, but not meals. This tour is $1,400.

3. **West Coast City and Outdoors Tour**
   On this tour, you'll go skiing outside of Denver. You'll also take a ride in a helicopter over the Grand Canyon, and climb mountains in California. You will see Los Angeles, visit the movie studios in Hollywood, and take a cable car in San Francisco. The tour is for seven days. You will stay in good-quality hotels. The hotels are included in the price of $1,900, but meals are extra.

INFORMATION GAP **Planning a Trip**

partner's name

STUDENT B | Work with a partner. One of you works on this page. The other works on page 5. Don't look at your partner's page.

Part One

In this episode, Kevin begins planning for his trip to San Francisco. Now your partner is planning a trip. Read the information on these three tours to the eastern part of the United States. Your partner will ask you questions about the tour. Help him/her find the best tour.

1. **East Coast Museum Tour**
   This tour takes you to the great museums of the East Coast. You'll go to museums in Boston, Philadelphia, New York, and Washington, D.C. You'll spend your entire day in museums and galleries with your guide. At night, you'll go to the best restaurants, and you'll stay at the best hotels. Hotel and meals are included in the price. The tour lasts one week. The cost is $2,500.

2. **Historic East Coast Tour**
   Visit important places in the history of the United States. You will visit Boston, Philadelphia, and Washington, D.C. with your guide. You have a free day in each place to visit museums or to shop. You'll stay in good-quality hotels. The hotel is included in the price, but meals are an additional cost. The tour lasts six days. The cost is $1,200.

3. **See the East Coast!**
   This tour takes you to historical places and museums on the East Coast. A guide takes you to the top sites. You will visit New York, Philadelphia, and Washington, D.C. You will stay in hotels that are not expensive. The price includes hotels, but meals are extra. The tour lasts 7 days. The cost is $1,000.

Part Two

Now it's your turn to plan a trip! Talk to a travel agent. Find out the best tour for you.

You want to take a tour of San Francisco and the western part of the United States. You like to do things outdoors, but you also want to visit some big cities. Your partner is a travel agent. You don't want to spend more than $2,000 for the tour. You want to stay at least one week. Your partner has some tours to sell. Ask questions about the tours. Decide which one is best for you. Write its number in the space below.

San Francisco

Ask questions like these:
- *What places does the tour go to?*
- *What things do you do with the tour group?*
- *How long is the tour?*
- *How much does the tour cost? What is included in the cost?*

Number of the tour you will take: _____

Friendship

EPISODE **46**

THEMES
- Being Impressed
- Collecting Autographs
- Sharing Good News

GAME
- The Music Business

OPTIONAL PROJECT
- Languages (Appendix 10)

THEME **Being Impressed**

| **1** | PARTNER | RANKING |

In this episode, Rebecca takes Kevin to the recording studio. He is very impressed with it. What kinds of things impress *you*?

A. Look at the choices below. Check (✔) the six things that impress you the most.

B. Then, ask your partner this question: *Which six things impress you the most?* Check (✔) your partner's answers.

partner's name

Oh, Rebecca, that was totally cool!

	You	Your partner
1. great art		
2. modern hospitals		
3. space travel		
4. computer technology		
5. the pyramids of Egypt		
6. the Great Wall of China		
7. people who can draw well		
8. people who can speak several languages		
9. great athletes		
10. great musicians		
11. great writers		
12. other: _____		

People do many things to impress others. Discuss the list below with your classmates. Add any other ideas that you can think of. Your teacher will write a "master list" on the board.

- dress well
- talk about interesting things you have done
- talk about your family
- talk about your accomplishments

- be early for an appointment
- talk about the money you have
- talk about your hobbies or interests
- talk about the latest films, songs, and so on

_____   _____

_____   _____

_____   _____

_____   _____

_____   _____

_____
partner's name

A. Work with a partner. One of you will be *Partner A*, the other will be *Partner B*. Follow the directions for each partner below.

Partner A: Write four things that you would do to impress a new friend. Use the list above in Activity 2.

1. _____
2. _____
3. _____
4. _____

Partner B: Write four things that a new friend could do that would impress you. Use the list above in Activity 2.

1. _____
2. _____
3. _____
4. _____

B. Compare answers. Do any of the items match?

1. When have you impressed somebody?
2. How did you know the person was impressed?
3. When were you last impressed? What impressed you?
4. What does *not* impress you?

THEME Collecting Autographs

4 **GROUP** **DISCUSSION**

group number

In this episode, Alex is very excited to receive an autographed baseball. It has the signatures of some professional baseball players on it.

Many people like to collect autographs. Who do people usually ask for their autographs? With your group, add items to the chart below.

People who give autographs	
Category	Names
Professional athletes	Michael Jordan, Monica Seles
1.	
2.	
3.	
4.	
5.	
6.	
7.	
8.	

5 **CLASS** **GAME** **Time: 10 min.**

Think of one interesting or unusual thing that you have done. Your classmates should not know about it. For example, did you ever have a small part in a movie? Did you ever meet a famous person? Did you ever win a prize?

A. On a piece of paper, write your name and what you did. Give your teacher the paper. Your teacher will choose *ten* interesting things and write them on the board. Copy any *five* of these onto a piece of paper.

B. Go around the class and try to find the person who did each of the five things on your list. Start your questions in the following way: *Did you ever. . .?* You can ask a person only one question at each exchange.

C. When you find a match, ask the person for his/her autograph. He or she will write it on your paper.

D. When you have an "autograph" for all five of the things on your paper, tell your teacher. You are the winner.

What About YOU?

1. Are you interested in collecting autographs?
2. Have you ever asked anyone for his/her autograph? Who?
3. Whose autograph would you like to have?

THEME Sharing Good News

In this episode, Bill shares his good news with Rebecca. He's going to Los Angeles to work as a musician. Here are some ways to talk about good news:

A	B
To announce good news	**To react to good news**
I have some good news.	That's great!
Listen, I've got something to tell you.	What wonderful news!
Guess what?	I'm so glad to hear it!
Listen to this!	Good for you!
	Terrific!

Work with a partner. Look at the situations below. Take turns. One partner announces some good news with an expression from Column **A** above.
The other partner reacts to the news with an expression from Column **B** above.
Then, make up your own situation.

EXAMPLE   You passed all your exams.
               Student A: Guess what?   Student B: Good for you!
                          I passed all my exams.

1. You've just won a new car.

Student A _____

Student B _____

2. You've just been accepted to a school.

Student A _____

Student B _____

3. You've just decided to get married.

Student A _____

Student B _____

4. Your situation:

Student A _____

Student B _____

Sit in a circle. One person begins the game by saying, "I have some good news.
I won fifty thousand dollars in the lottery." The next person answers, "That's great!"
He/she then repeats all the good news and adds something new: "I have some
good news. I won fifty thousand dollars in the lottery and I just bought a new car."
How many pieces of good news can your group list before someone forgets?

GAME **The Music Business**

What do you know about the music business? Play this music tic-tac-toe game and find out.

Get Ready to Play

Step One
Divide into four teams. Team 1 will play Team 2, and Team 3 will play Team 4.

Step Two
Each team will write 10 questions about songs and musicians. The questions must begin with *Who sings the song. . .?* or *Who sang the song. . .?* Then, you must give three answer choices.

EXAMPLES

Who sings the song, "Dream Catcher"?
  a. Julio Iglesias
  b. Madonna
  c. Rebecca Casey

Who sang the song, "Yesterday"?
  a. The Rolling Stones
  b. The Beatles
  c. Juan Luis Guerra

Write your questions below:

1. _____
  a. _____
  b. _____
  c. _____

2. _____
  a. _____
  b. _____
  c. _____

3. _____
  a. _____
  b. _____
  c. _____

4. _____
  a. _____
  b. _____
  c. _____

5. _____
  a. _____
  b. _____
  c. _____

6. _____
  a. _____
  b. _____
  c. _____

7. _____
  a. _____
  b. _____
  c. _____

8. _____
  a. _____
  b. _____
  c. _____

9. _____
  a. _____
  b. _____
  c. _____

10. _____
  a. _____
  b. _____
  c. _____

GAME The Music Business

Step Three

Decide which team will be the Os and which team will be the Xs. Flip a coin to see which team goes first.

Step Four

Cut out the game pieces on Appendix 13. The O team will cut out the Os and the X team will cut out the Xs. Now you're ready to play.

Play the Game

- The O team asks the X team a music question. If the X team answers the question correctly, it gets to put an X in one of the tic-tac-toe squares below.
- If the X team doesn't answer the question correctly, it doesn't get to mark a square, and it's the O team's turn.
- Take turns asking questions. The first team to get three X's or three O's in a row or diagonally wins! Play several rounds of the game. Write new questions if necessary.

The Lost Boys

EPISODE **47**

THEMES
- Changing Plans
- Baby-sitting
- Children and Money

INFORMATION GAP
- A Missing Person's Report

OPTIONAL PROJECT
- Ice Skating (Appendix 11)

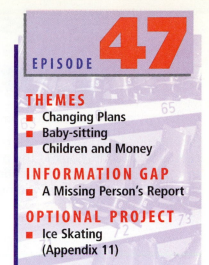

THEME **Changing Plans**

| **1** | **PARTNER** | **INTERVIEW** | |

partner's name

In this episode, Alex and Vincent are lost. Kevin and Rebecca change their plans to help look for the boys. Some people can change plans more easily than others. These people are more flexible.

Read the situations below. Decide if you would change your plans. Check (✔) *Yes* or *No*. Then, ask your partner about the situations. Check (✔) your partner's answers. Who is more flexible?

	WOULD YOU CHANGE YOUR PLANS?			
	You		**Your partner**	
	Yes	No	Yes	No
1. You have tickets to the theater. Someone in your family is ill.				
2. You plan to take tomorrow off to visit your child's school. Your boss wants you to go to an important meeting.				
3. You're going to go to the beach for a week-long vacation. You break your leg.				
4. You're going to go shopping to buy a special present for a friend. You have a fight with this friend.				
5. You want to get to a store before it closes. You see a small child in the street. He/she looks lost.				

 What About YOU?

1. Do you change your plans often?
2. Are there any situations when you should not change plans? What are they?
3. How do you feel if a friend cancels plans to do something with you?
4. Do you like to make plans?

THEME Baby-sitting

In this episode, a baby-sitter comes to take care of Alex.

Parents need to give baby-sitters clear instructions. You have a four-year-old child named John. Look at the picture. Work with your group. Use the clues in it to complete the list of instructions for the baby-sitter. Continue the list on a separate piece of paper if you need to. Add any other instructions you think are important.

List of Instructions
1. If there's a problem, call us at the party. The number is next to the phone.
2. You can read books to John.
3. John shouldn't touch the computer.
_____
_____
_____
_____
_____

What About YOU?

1. In the United States, teenagers often baby-sit to make money. Do teenagers do this in your country?
2. If yes, how much money do baby-sitters earn in your country?
3. Did you ever baby-sit to make money?

THEME Children and Money

In this episode, Vincent takes the money out of his piggy bank. Mrs. Wang finds his empty bank. Children in the United States often have piggy banks. They put money they want to save into their piggy banks.

In this puzzle, you need to figure out the kinds of coins in each piggy bank. Work with a partner. Write your answers in the boxes.

1¢	5¢	10¢	25¢	50¢
penny	nickel	dime	quarter	half dollar

Alex has 6¢ in his piggy bank.
He has two coins.

Answer 1 nickel, 1 penny
5¢ + 1¢ = 6¢

1. Marta has 77¢ in her piggy bank.
   She has five coins.

   Answer

2. Lisa has 95¢ in her piggy bank.
   She has 11 coins.

   Answer

3. Motoi has 53¢ in his piggy bank.
   He has seven coins.

   Answer

4. Peter has 66¢ in his piggy bank.
   He has four coins.

   Answer

Bonus Question

Alex has 51¢ in his piggy bank. He only has one penny. How many coin combinations are possible?
Think of as many as you can.
Use a separate piece of paper if necessary.

Combinations

1. one half dollar + one penny
2. two quarters + one penny

In the United States and Canada, children often have their own money to spend. What is usual in your country? Did you have your own money as a child? Check (✔) your answers to the questions below. Then, ask your partner, and check (✔) your partner's answers.

	You	Your partner
1. In your country, how many children have their own money?	❑ most ❑ some ❑ few	❑ most ❑ some ❑ few
2. Where do children get money?	❑ from their parents ❑ as gifts ❑ from working ❑ other _____	❑ from their parents ❑ as gifts ❑ from working ❑ other _____
3. What do children usually do with their money?	❑ spend it for fun ❑ use it for necessities ❑ save it for the future	❑ spend it for fun ❑ use it for necessities ❑ save it for the future
4. How much spending money did you have as a child?	❑ lots ❑ some ❑ little	❑ lots ❑ some ❑ little
5. Who decided how you used your money?	❑ I did. ❑ My parents did. ❑ other _____	❑ I did. ❑ My parents did. ❑ other _____

5 | **PARTNER** | **ROLE-PLAY**

partner's name

A. With your partner, act out a conversation between a child and a parent. One of you takes the role of the child. The other takes the role of the parent. Read your positions in the boxes below.

B. Do one conversation. Then, change roles.

C. Volunteer to perform your role-play in front of the class.

Child

Your parent gives you a little money each week. This is your allowance. You would like a bigger allowance. Try to persuade your parent to increase your allowance. You can:
- _explain why you need the money_
- _offer to earn the money_
- _tell how much your friends get each week_

Parent

You give your child some money every week. You want your child to learn the value of money. You want your child to learn not to spend more money than he/she has. Also, you yourself are trying to save money to buy a new car. Listen to your child. Make a decision.
- _Does your child have a real need for the money?_
- _Does your child offer to earn the money?_
- _Does your child show he/she is learning the value of money?_

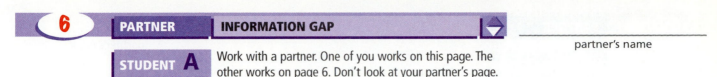

6	**PARTNER**	**INFORMATION GAP**	

partner's name

STUDENT A — Work with a partner. One of you works on this page. The other works on page 6. Don't look at your partner's page.

Someday, you may have to describe someone who is missing. How well can you describe a person? To do this activity, bring a photo of a person to class. It may be from a magazine. It may be someone you know. The teacher will collect the photos and place them face down on a table or a desk. Before you begin, pick a photo. Make sure it isn't the one you brought in. Don't show it to anyone else.

Part One

Study the photo for one minute. Then turn it over. Your partner needs to get a description of the "missing person." Describe the person in the photo as carefully as you can, but don't look at the photo again! Talk about what the person is wearing and what he/she looks like. Your partner will take notes. He/she will also ask questions.

Part Two

Your partner will look at a photo of a "missing person" for one minute. You need to get information about the missing person. Fill in the form below. First, your partner will give a description. Then, ask questions about the person.

MISSING PERSON'S REPORT

Age _____   Sex (M/F) _____

Height _____   Weight _____

Hair color _____   Eye color _____

Clothing _____

Other information _____

_____

_____

_____

Part Three

Return your photo to the teacher. The teacher will number all of the photos and put them on display. Can you find the missing person your partner described? Check your guess with your partner. Then, compare your missing person's report with your partner's. Answer these questions:

- *Who remembered the most about his/her photo?*
- *What kinds of things did you notice about the person in the photo?*
- *What kinds of things didn't you notice?*

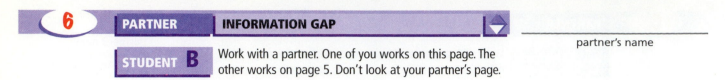

STUDENT **B**   Work with a partner. One of you works on this page. The other works on page 5. Don't look at your partner's page.

Someday, you may have to describe someone who is missing. How well can you describe a person? To do this activity, bring a photo of a person to class. It may be from a magazine. It may be someone you know. The teacher will collect the photos and place them face down on a table or a desk. Before you begin, pick a photo. Make sure it isn't the one you brought in. Don't show it to anyone else.

Part One

Your partner will look at a photo of a "missing person" for one minute.
You need to get information about the missing person. Fill in the form below.
First, your partner will give a description. Then, ask questions about the person.

MISSING PERSON'S REPORT

Age _____   Sex (M/F) _____

Height _____   Weight _____

Hair color _____   Eye color _____

Clothing _____

Other information _____

_____

_____

_____

Part Two

Study the photo you have for one minute. Then turn it over. Your partner needs to get a description of the "missing person." Describe the person in the photo as carefully as you can, but don't look at the photo again! Talk about what the person is wearing and what he/she looks like. Your partner will take notes. He/she will also ask questions.

Part Three

Return your photo to the teacher. The teacher will number all of the photos and put them on display. Can you find the missing person your partner described? Check your guess with your partner. Then, compare your missing person's report with your partner's. Answer these questions:
- *Who remembered the most about his/her photo?*
- *What kinds of things did you notice about the person in the photo?*
- *What kinds of things didn't you notice?*

A Very Good Year

EPISODE **48**

THEMES
- New Year's Resolutions
- Trust
- Parenting

GAME
- Grounding

OPTIONAL PROJECT
- New Year's Eve (Appendix 12)

THEME New Year's Resolutions

| 1 | PARTNER | INTERVIEW | ▲ |

_____
partner's name

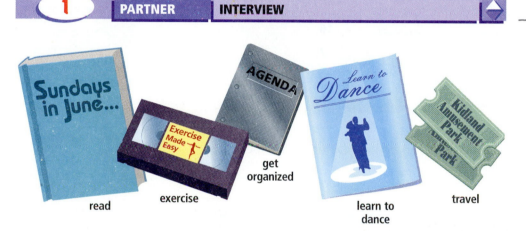

read   exercise   get organized   learn to dance   travel

At New Year's time, people often make promises about what they will do during the new year. These promises are called **New Year's resolutions**. Here are some examples:

I will get organized.	I will learn to dance.	I will eat less junk food.
I will travel.	I will exercise more.	I will read more.

Work with a partner. Pretend it's New Year's Eve.

A. Write three New Year's resolutions in the spaces below. You can use the examples in the box above, or you can think of others.

B. Ask your partner the question: *What are your New Year's resolutions?* Write your partner's answers.

Your New Year's resolutions

1. _____
2. _____
3. _____

Your partner's New Year's resolutions

1. _____
2. _____
3. _____

A. Write one of your three New Year's resolutions from Activity 1 on a small piece of paper. Don't write your name on it, and don't show it to anyone.

B. Give your paper to the teacher. The teacher will number each resolution by writing a number in the corner of each paper. Then, he/she will put them on a table or desk.

C. With your classmates, look at all the cards. Try to guess who wrote each resolution. Write your guesses below.

Resolution number	Person		Resolution number	Person
1.	_____		11.	_____
2.	_____		12.	_____
3.	_____		13.	_____
4.	_____		14.	_____
5.	_____		15.	_____
6.	_____		16.	_____
7.	_____		17.	_____
8.	_____		18.	_____
9.	_____		19.	_____
10.	_____		20.	_____

D. When the time is up, each person tells which is his/her resolution. The person with the most correct guesses wins.

3   **CLASS**   **DISCUSSION**

Your English class is a good place for a New Year's resolution!

Each person in the class will make one resolution about learning English. Your teacher can help you with your resolution.

Here are some examples of good resolutions:	Write your resolution here. Then share it with the class.
I will speak English outside of class with classmates. I will read English on my own at least two hours a week.	_____ _____

What About YOU?

1. Do you ever make New Year's resolutions?
2. Do you always *keep* your resolutions?
3. How many resolutions do you think a person should make?

THEME Trust

4 **PARTNER** **TRUST TEST**

_____
partner's name

Take this "Trust Test." Read the situations. Check (✔) *Yes* or *No*. Then ask your partner the questions, and check (✔) your partner's answers. Discuss the results.

	You		Your partner	
	Yes	No	Yes	No
1. You sometimes lend things to a friend. She doesn't give them back. Then she asks to borrow your new CD and promises to give it back. Do you trust her?				
2. Your mechanic promised to fix your car yesterday. Now he says it will be ready today. Do you trust him?				
3. Someone you just met didn't keep an appointment with you. You waited an hour. Now he wants to make another appointment. Do you trust him to keep it?				
4. You have a new car. Your brother, who is very careful, asks to borrow it. Do you trust him enough to let him use it?				
5. Your boyfriend/girlfriend asks you to lend him/her some money. Do you trust him/her to return it?				
6. The television repair person has promised to come and fix your TV today. Do you believe her?				
7. You have some valuable jewelry. You don't want to leave it in your apartment when you are away on vacation. Do you trust a friend to keep it for you?				
8. Someone on the street offers to sell you gold jewelry at a low price. Do you trust him?				
9. Someone calls you on the phone and says you have won a boat. Do you trust him?				

SCORING: *Yes answers are worth 1 point.*
No answers are worth 0 points.

If your score is 1 point or lower: You aren't very trusting.

If your score is between 2–6 points: You're in the middle. You trust some people, but you don't believe everything people tell you.

If your score is 7 points or more: You're too trusting. You shouldn't believe everything people tell you.

THEME Parenting

Pretend you have an eight-year-old child.

A. What answers do you give in the following situations? Circle them in the chart below. *Note: "I'll think about it" means you may or may not agree. Often it suggests you won't say yes.*

B. Find out your partner's answers. Ask this question: *What would you say?* Circle your partner's answers.

C. Who is more strict—you or your partner? If you're strict, you'll say no more often.

You			Situation	Your partner		
Yes	No	I'll think about it.	1. Your child asks for $20 for a video.	Yes	No	I'll think about it.
Yes	No	I'll think about it.	2. Your child asks for an expensive game. He/she says everyone in the school has it.	Yes	No	I'll think about it.
Yes	No	I'll think about it.	3. Your child wants to go with a 10-year-old friend to an ice-skating rink across town.	Yes	No	I'll think about it.
Yes	No	I'll think about it.	4. Your child asks to go on a ride at an amusement park. The ride isn't recommended for children under 10.	Yes	No	I'll think about it.
Yes	No	I'll think about it.	5. Your child asks to go to a movie. All his/her friends have seen it. The newspaper says it's scary for children under 10.	Yes	No	I'll think about it.

A. Read the two opinions below. If you agree with Opinion 1, join group 1. If you agree with Opinion 2, join Group 2.

B. With your group members, make a list of reasons to support your opinion. Be ready to explain each one. Use a separate piece of paper.

C. Take turns. Each group has five minutes to present its ideas.

D. Discuss the opinion most of the class agrees with.

Opinion 1	Opinion 2
It's better to be strict with your children. If you're too relaxed, there'll be trouble.	It's better to be relaxed, with your children. If you're too strict, there'll be trouble.

Write your reasons on a separate piece of paper.

GAME **Grounding**

In this episode, Ramón **grounds** his son. This means that Alex can't go out and play with his friends for a period of time. It's a common way to punish children in the United States. Play this game and decide how *you* would punish *your* children.

You know you're grounded, right?

Play the Game

■ Form a team of four people. Then divide your team into two sets of partners.

■ Work with your partner. Look at the list of bad behaviors on page 6. Discuss each behavior, and decide on one of five punishments. Check (✔) your answers in the chart on page 6. Don't show your answers to the other half of your team!

EXAMPLE   Your child fought at school.

	Grounding for two weeks	Grounding for one week	Extra house work	No dessert after dinner	No punishment
Bad behavior 1		✔			
Bad behavior 2					

You think your child should be grounded for one week for fighting in school.

■ When you've finished, join the other half of your team. Compare answers. Your team gets a point if both parts of a team have checked the same punishment for the same bad behavior.

■ A total of 12 points is possible. The team with the most points wins. Keep track of your points in the chart below.

Game Rules

■ Groups cannot change any answers after they have checked them. After you check all 12 answers, put down your pens and pencils.

■ Don't talk to the other group in your team until after you both have finished all 12 answers.

	Points
Bad behavior 1	
Bad behavior 2	
Bad behavior 3	
Bad behavior 4	
Bad behavior 5	
Bad behavior 6	
Bad behavior 7	
Bad behavior 8	
Bad behavior 9	
Bad behavior 10	
Bad behavior 11	
Bad behavior 12	

GAME Grounding

Bad Behaviors
1. Your child got bad grades in school.
2. Your child cheated at school.
3. Your child fought at school.
4. Your child lied to you.
5. Your child hit his/her brother/sister.
6. Your child ran away.
7. Your child stole money from you.
8. Your child stole money from a store.
9. Your child used bad language.
10. Your child was mean to the dog.
11. Your child broke a window with a ball.
12. Your child spilled milk on your favorite book.

Check (✔) your answers.

	Grounding for two weeks	Grounding for one week	Extra house work	No dessert after dinner	No punishment
Bad behavior 1					
Bad behavior 2					
Bad behavior 3					
Bad behavior 4					
Bad behavior 5					
Bad behavior 6					
Bad behavior 7					
Bad behavior 8					
Bad behavior 9					
Bad behavior 10					
Bad behavior 11					
Bad behavior 12					

Keep track of your points on page 5.

EPISODE **37**

PROJECT **Computer Classes**

1 GROUP RESEARCH

In this episode, Kevin talks to Michael about computer classes.

A. Divide into groups. Call or visit a college, university, or computer institute in your area. Each group should try to choose a different school. Ask the questions below. Write the answers on a separate piece of paper.

1. How many computer classes does the school offer?
2. What kinds of computer classes are they?
3. How much do the classes cost?

B. Compare your answers with the class. List the four most common types of classes. Then, vote on the best place to take computer classes.

1. _____   3. _____

2. _____   4. _____

2 GROUP SURVEY

group number

Work in the same groups from Activity 1. Your group wants to open a computer school. You need to get some information. Who would come to your school? Which classes would be most popular?

A. Each person in the group needs to talk to three people outside the class. Complete an interview card like the one below for each person. List the four kinds of courses from Activity 1.

> Name _____   Age _____   Sex _____
>
> **1.** Do you use a computer now?   Yes ☐ No ☐
> **2.** Do you want to take computer classes?   Yes ☐ No ☐
> **3.** If yes, what kind of computer class do you want to take?
>   Would you take ... (classes from Activity 1, Part B)
>   1. _____ Yes ☐ No ☐   3. _____ Yes ☐ No ☐
>   2. _____ Yes ☐ No ☐   4. _____ Yes ☐ No ☐

B. Compare the surveys in your group. Complete the information below.

1. Who gave more "Yes" answers, men or women? _____
2. How many "Yes" answers did the following age groups have?

   10–20 years _____   21–29 years _____   30–49 years _____   50+ years _____

3. Which classes would be the most popular at your school? _____

 What About YOU?
1. Do you use a computer regularly?
2. If so, why do you use the computer?
3. If not, would you like to use a computer? Why or why not?
4. What kinds of computer classes would you like to take?

EPISODE 38

PROJECT Sports for Children

 PARTNER **SURVEY**

In this episode, we see Alex and his friends kicking a soccer ball. The children are playing sports in their after-school program.

You're going to help your local community center. It wants to start an after-school sports program for children. Because of money, it can start the program with only two sports. You're getting information to help the center choose the two sports. Your teacher will divide the class into an even number of pairs. Half of the pairs will do Activity A and half of the pairs will do Activity B.

Activity A

With your partner, interview at least three children from the ages of 6–12. Ask the following questions and write their answers in the chart. Continue the chart on a separate piece of paper if necessary.

- *What team sport do you like to play the most?*
- *What individual sport do you like to play the most?*

Child	Team sport	Individual sport
1		
2		
3		

Activity B

With your partner, interview at least three parents of children of the ages of 6–12. Ask the following questions and write their answers in the chart. Continue the chart on a separate piece of paper if necessary.

- *What team sport do you think is best for your children to play?*
- *What individual sport do you think is best for your children to play?*
- *Which are better for your children to play—team sports or individual sports?*

Parent	Team sport	Individual sport	Which are better—team or individual sports?
1			
2			
3			

A. Join a pair that did a different activity from the one you did. Discuss the answers to both surveys. What conclusions can you make?

B. Share your information with the rest of the class. What sports will you recommend to the community center?

EPISODE 39

PROJECT Opera

1   PARTNER   RESEARCH

In this episode, Alberto wants Rebecca to go to the opera with him.

In operas, singing and music tell a story. Grand opera is sung in opera houses around the world. Great composers like Mozart, Verdi, and Wagner wrote grand opera in the 1700s and 1800s.

There are other musical styles used to tell stories. For example, there are rock operas. In English-speaking countries, there is a popular form of storytelling through songs. It's called a musical. You may have heard of musicals like "Cats" or "Phantom of the Opera." Many cultures have their own special forms of musical storytelling.

Work with a partner. Find the name of an opera or a musical. Pick one you would like to know more about. To get names and information, you can interview people, look at music encyclopedias, or go to a music store. Complete the following chart. Be prepared to tell the story of the musical to the class.

> Name of opera or musical _____
>
> Who wrote it _____ When it was written _____
>
> The main characters _____
>
> _____
>
> The main story _____
>
> _____
>
> _____
>
> What happens at the end _____
>
> _____
>
> _____

2   CLASS   STORYTELLING

A. With your partner from Activity 1, make a presentation to the class. Write the name of the opera or musical on the board. Share your information about it. If possible, play parts of it to the class.

B. When all the presentations are finished, discuss these questions:
   - *Which was the most unusual fact you learned?*
   - *Which story seems the most interesting?*

C. Have the class members vote for the opera or musical that they would like to see the most. They can also vote on the opera or musical that they would *not* want to see.

EPISODE 40

PROJECT **Using the Library**

A. Divide into groups. Work together to answer the questions below about your local or school libraries. If possible, each group should call or visit a different library. Use a separate piece of paper to write your answers.

1. When is the library open?
2. What do you have to do to borrow books?
3. How do you find the books you want?
4. How do you find the magazines the library has?
5. What does the library have besides books and magazines?
6. Does the library have Internet access?
7. What are three magazines you can read at the library?
8. What are three reference books you can use at the library?

B. When each group is finished, compare answers as a class. Which library would be the best place to do research?

partner's name

A. Work with a partner. Do library research to answer the following questions. Write your answers in the chart. Write where you found the information and how long it took you to find it. Don't forget to try the Internet.

Questions	Answers	Where you found the information	Time
1. What is the capital city of Niger?			
2. Who was the fourth president of the United States? When did he become president?			
3. Who are two actors who played in the movie *Star Wars*?			
4. What was the first year that women were allowed to compete in the Olympic Games?			
5. Where is the Rock and Roll Hall of Fame? When did it open?			

B. Compare answers as a class. Which pairs found the most correct answers most quickly? Which sources did they use?

EPISODE 41

PROJECT Vemcations

| 1 | PARTNER | RESEARCH |

partner's name

In this episode, Alberto is planning a ski vacation in Colorado. Where would you like to go on vacation?

A. With a partner, decide on a place you would like to visit.

B. Find out about the place. You can go to a travel agent and get information and brochures. Or you can go to the library to look at travel books and magazines. You can also get information on the Internet. Try to find some pictures.

C. Answer the following questions.

1. Where would you like to go? _____

2. How would you get there? _____

3. Where would you stay? _____

4. What kind of weather should you expect? _____

5. How much would your vacation cost? _____

6. What would you do there? _____

_____

_____

_____

_____

_____

_____

_____

| 2 | PARTNER | PRESENTATION |

partner's name

A. With your partner from Activity 1, make a presentation to the class. Write the name of the vacation place on the board. Share your information about this place. Tell why you want to go there. Try to show your classmates that this is a great place to visit. Show pictures of your place if you can.

B. When all the presentations are finished, take a class vote. Each person will answer the question: *Which place would you like to visit?* Vote for one place—it can't be the one that you researched. The teacher will write the results of the vote on the board.

1. What do you usually do on vacation?
2. What is your favorite vacation memory?
3. Have you ever taken a ski vacation? If yes, where did you go? If no, would like to take a ski vacation?

EPISODE 42

PROJECT Dedication

1	PARTNER	RESEARCH	

_____
partner's name

Right now, it's got to be my music... and my music alone.

Rebecca is dedicated to her music. She will do anything necessary to be a songwriter and performer.

A. Work with a partner. Choose any dedicated person in the history of the world. This person can be alive or dead, famous or not famous. Here are some examples:

Nelson Mandela	Louis Pasteur
Dian Fossey	Maria Taglioni
Leo Tolstoy	Mahatma Gandhi
Katharine Hepburn	Elizabeth Cady Stanton
Simón Bolívar	

B. Complete the information below. You can use your school library, a biographical dictionary, an encyclopedia, the Internet, and so on.

Name of the dedicated person _____

_____

_____

_____

Where the person was/is from _____

_____

_____

_____

What the person was dedicated to _____

_____

_____

_____

What the person accomplished _____

_____

_____

_____

C. Present the information to the class. Show a picture of the person if possible.

1. If you could meet one of the people from Activity 1, who would it be?
2. Why would you want to meet this person?
3. What are you dedicated to?
4. What have you accomplished?

EPISODE 43

PROJECT Chocolates

 1 **PARTNER** **RESEARCH**

_____
partner's name

In this episode, Nancy and Rebecca eat chocolate. What do you know about chocolate?

A. With your partner, find the answers to the following questions. You can use your school library, an encyclopedia, the Internet, and so on. You can also go to a candy store to get some help! Write your answers on a separate piece of paper.

1. From what tree is chocolate made?
2. Which cultures first used chocolate?
3. In which country do people eat the most chocolate?
4. What are four kinds of chocolate?

When you finish, compare your answers as a class. How many different kinds of chocolate can the class list?

 2 **GROUP** **SURVEY**

_____
group number

In the United States and Canada, giving boxes of chocolates is a tradition on Valentine's Day. This holiday celebrates love and romance. People give gifts of chocolates and other candies on other holidays, too, such as Christmas, Easter, and Halloween.

A. Find out about customs in other countries. Interview people in your group and people outside of class. Ask these questions:
- _Are gifts of chocolates or other candies popular on holidays?_
- _What is the name of the holiday?_
- _What is the custom that has to do with the chocolates or candies?_
  (Copy the chart below onto another piece of paper, and add extra lines.)

B. Share your findings with the class.

Country	Holiday	The custom
1. the United States	Halloween	Children dress in costumes. They go to friends' or neighbors' doors and say, "Trick or treat." They usually get some candy.
2.		
3.		

1. In your country, are chocolates a popular treat?
2. Do people give chocolates as gifts?
3. Do you like to eat chocolates?

EPISODE 44

PROJECT Helping People in the Community

	GROUP	RESEARCH	

group number

In this episode, Ramón and Rebecca help people in their community. They help serve food at the community center. How can you help people in your community?

A. With your group members, find out about a local program/organization that helps your community in one of the following areas:

Education	Housing
Food and Nutrition	The Environment
Parenthood and Family	Services for the Elderly
Disease and Disability	Sports and Athletics
Services for Immigrants	Bad Weather/Natural Disasters

B. Use your school library, a newspaper, the Internet, and so on. You can also call or visit local government offices, community centers, or volunteer organizations. Answer the following questions about your program/organization. Use a separate piece of paper.
   1. What's the name of the program/organization?
   2. Where is it located?
   3. What services does the program/organization offer?
   4. What can volunteers do there?

C. Present your information to the class. Explain why your program/organization is important to the community. Also, explain why it would be fun to volunteer there.

D. As a class, choose one of the programs/organizations from the presentations. Plan a volunteer activity for the whole class with that program/organization. Take a lot of of photos! After the volunteer activity, show the photos to the principal/director of your school and tell him/her about what you did.

1. Besides this project, have you ever helped people in your community? What did you do?
2. Have people in your community ever helped you? What did they do?
3. What do you think the most helpful community program is in your area?

EPISODE 45

PROJECT Legends

1 GROUP RESEARCH

In this episode, Ramón tells Rebecca about the legend of the ekeko. A legend is a kind of story from the past. Usually the stories in legends never happened. Often legends contain magic or mysterious events. Most cultures have legends. Some legends are about how the world began. Some legends are about heroes. Some are about lovers.

Legend has it that he can bring you good luck and fulfill your dreams. You hang all your dreams on the ekeko, and they'll come true.

Atlantis	El Dorado	The Holy Grail
King Arthur	The Flying Dutchman	Pandora's Box
Quetzalcóatl	Paul Bunyan	John Henry
	El Cid	

Your legend _____

Divide into groups. Choose a person, event, object, or place from the list above, or think of your own. Find out about its legend. Write about the legend below. Tell the story of the legend. You can use your school library, an encyclopedia, the Internet, and so on.

Legend _____

_____

_____

_____

_____

_____

_____

_____

_____

2 GROUP POSTER

Work in the same groups from Activity 1. If possible, get colored paper, colored pencils, markers, and so on. Make a poster of your legend. Write a description of your legend on your poster. Present it to the class and tell the story of the legend.

What About YOU?

1. Why do people like legends?
2. What was the first legend you ever learned about?
3. What's your favorite legend?

EPISODE 46

PROJECT Languages

---

1   **GROUP**   **RESEARCH**

group number

In this episode, Vincent and Alex talk about the languages of Taiwan (Mandarin) and Mexico (Spanish). What do you know about the languages of the world?

Work with a partner. Answer the questions below about languages. You can use the school library, an encyclopedia, an almanac, the Internet, and so on. When you finish, compare your answers with those of another group.

1 Do they speak English there?

2 I don't know. I think they speak Mandarin.

1. How many languages (and dialects) are there in the world? Check (✔) your answer.

   A. under 10,000 _____   B. 10,000–20,000 _____   C. over 20,000 _____

2. Put the following languages in order from 1–10. Write *1* next to the language that the most people speak, write *2* next to the language that is the second most commonly spoken, and so on.

   _____ Arabic   _____ Chinese (Mandarin)   _____ German   _____ Japanese   _____ Russian

   _____ Bengali   _____ English   _____ Hindi   _____ Portuguese   _____ Spanish

3. Over one billion people (1,000,000,000) speak Chinese! How many people speak the language(s) in the list below?

   French _____   Urdu _____

   Thai _____   Tagalog _____

---

2   **TEAM**   **GAME**

team number

How many words from different languages can you find?

A. Divide into teams. Copy the chart below onto a separate piece of paper. Add more lines.

B. Walk around your school, campus, or neigborhood. Find words from as many different languages as you can. Look at signs, posters, and books. Write the words below. Next to these words, write what language they are from, and what they mean in English. *(Note: Use each language only once.)*

C. Share your answers with your classmates. The team with the longest list wins.

	Word	Language	Definition in English
EXAMPLE	adiós	Spanish	goodbye
1.			
2.			
3.			

EPISODE 47

PROJECT Ice Skating

---

1 **PARTNER** **RESEARCH**

_____
partner's name

What do you know about ice skating? Work with a partner. Your teacher will assign you one of the questions below. Find the answers using your school library, an encyclopedia, the Internet, and so on. Write your answers on a separate piece of paper. Share your answers with the class.

1. What are the differences between speed skating and figure skating?
2. When was speed skating first included in the Olympics?
3. When was figure skating first included in the Olympics?
4. Who is a famous speed skater? Who is a famous figure skater?

---

2 **PARTNER** **RESEARCH**

_____
partner's name

Do one of the following activities. Present your findings to the class.

Activity A

Work with a partner. Choose one of the Olympic figure skaters from the list below. Find out the following information about this person.

1. What year did this person win a medal in the Olympics? _____
2. How old was this person when he/she won the medal? _____
3. What country is/was this person from? _____

Karl Schaefer	Sonja Henie	Oksana Baiul	Richard Button
Viktor Petrenko	Elizabeth Manley	Katarina Witt	Scott Hamilton

Activity B

Work with a partner. How fast is a speed skater? Find the Olympic records. Then, answer the questions below. Note: You will compare the speeds in different sports. You will compare the speeds over different distances.
You may have to do some math! Write the speeds on a separate piece of paper.

1. How fast can an Olympic speed skater travel 100 meters? 500 meters? 1,000 meters?
2. How fast can Olympic runners complete these distances? How fast do swimmers go? Find the speeds for various sports.

EPISODE 48

PROJECT New Year's Eve

 1 **PARTNER** **RESEARCH**

In this episode, Ramón, Rebecca, Kevin, and Alex celebrate New Year's Eve together.

Work with a partner. Find out about New Year's Eve celebrations for a country, culture, or religion that neither of you is familiar with. You can use your school library, an encyclopedia, the Internet, and so on. You can also interview people. Find out the answers to the following questions. Try to answer as many as you can.

New Year's Celebration

Place, Culture, or Religion _____

1. When is it celebrated? _____

2. Why is it celebrated on this date? _____
_____

3. What do people do? _____
_____

4. What are the reasons for these traditions? _____
_____

5. What do people eat and drink? _____
_____

6. Why do they eat these things? _____
_____

 2 **CLASS** **PRESENTATION**

With your partner from Activity 1, make a presentation to the class. Write the name of your place, culture, or religion on the board. Share your information about New Year's Eve.

When all the presentations are finished, discuss these questions as a class:
- *How are some of the New Year's celebrations alike?*
- *Which was the most unusual fact you learned?*
- *Which celebration would you like to join in the most?*

1. What do you usually do on New Year's Eve?
2. What's the most unusual thing you've ever done on New Year's Eve?
3. Have you ever spent New Year's Eve alone?

APPENDIX **13** **Manipulatives**

Episode 39

Episode 41

Clues

1. Susanna Sills's present is a sweater.
2. Carson Chills's present is a camera.
3. Ben Bills's present is a bat.
4. Thalia Tills's present is a ticket.

Episode 44

Episode 46